COLLECTED POEMS

COLLECTED POEMS

by

HERBERT READ

SINCLAIR-STEVENSON

First published in Great Britain by
Sinclair-Stevenson Limited
7/8 Kendrick Mews
London SW7 3HG
England

Copyright © 1926 Benedict Read

First published in Great Britain in 1966 by
Faber and Faber Limited

British Library Cataloguing in Publication Data

A CIP catalogue record for this book is available from the British Library.

ISBN 1 85619 132 X (hardback)
ISBN 1 85616 142 7 (paperback)

Printed and bound in Great Britain by
Biddles Limited, Guildford and King's Lynn

For
MARGARET

CONTENTS

8

9

NEW POEMS 1965

VOCAL AVOWALS

VOCAL AVOWALS

ECLOGUES
(1914–18)

I. MEDITATION OF A LOVER
AT DAYBREAK

I can just see the distant trees
and I wonder whether they will
    or will not
bow their tall plumes at your passing
in the carriage of the morning wind:

Or whether they will merely
tremble against the cold dawnlight,
shaking a yellow leaf
    to the dew-wet earth.

II. WOODLANDS

Pine needles cover the silent ground:
    pine trees chancel the woodland ways.

We penetrate into the dark depths
where only garlic and hemlock grow
till we meet the blue stream
cleaving the green
    twilight like a rhythmic sword.

III. PASTURELANDS

We scurry over the pastures
    chasing the windstrewn oak-leaves.

We kiss
the fresh petals of cowslips and primroses.

We discover frog-spawn in the wet ditch.

IV. THE POND

Shrill green weeds
float on the black pond.

A rising fish
   ripples the still water

And disturbs my soul.

V. THE ORCHARD

Grotesque patterns of blue-gray mould
cling to my barren apple-trees:
But in spring
pale blossoms break like flames
along black wavering twigs:
And soon
rains wash the cold frail petals
downfalling like tremulous flakes
even within my heart.

VI. APRIL

To the fresh wet fields
and the white
froth of flowers

Came the wild errant
swallows with a scream.

VII. THE WOODMAN

His russet coat and gleaming axe
flit
in the blue glades.

The wild birds sing
but the woodman he broods
in the blue glades.

VIII. HARVEST HOME

The wagons loom like blue caravans in the dusk:
they lumber mysteriously down the moonlit lanes.

We ride on the stacks of rust gold corn
filling the sky with our song.

The horses toss their heads and the harness-bells
jingle all the way.

IX. APPEAL

O dark eyes, I am weary
of the white wrath of the sea.

O come with me to the vernal woods
the green sap and the fragrant
white violets.

X. CURFEW

Like a faun my head uplifted
in delicate mists:

And breaking on my soul
tremulous waves that beat and cling
to yellow leaves and dark green hills:

Bells in the autumn evening.

XI. CHILDHOOD

I

The old elmtrees flock round the tiled farmstead; their silver-bellied leaves dance in the wind. Beneath their shade, in the corner of the Green, is a pond. In Winter it is full of water, green with weeds: in Spring a lily will open there.

The ducks waddle in the mud and sail in circles round the pond, or preen their feathers on the bank.

But in Summer the pond is dry, and its bed is glossy and baked by the sun, a beautiful soft colour like the skins of the moles they catch and crucify on the stable doors.

On the green the fowls pick grains, or chatter and fight. Their yellows, whites and browns, the metallic lustre of their darker feathers, and the crimson splash of their combs make an ever-changing pattern on the grass.

They drink with spasmodic upreaching necks by the side of the well.

Under the stones by the well live green lizards curious to our eyes.

The path from the well leads to a garden door set in the high wall whereon grow plums and apricots. The door is deep and narrow and opens on to paths bordered with box-hedges; one path leads through the aromatic currant bushes, beneath the plum-trees, to the lawn where grows the wonder of our day-dreams, the monkey's puzzle-tree. On the other side of the lawn three fir-trees rise sharply to the sky, their dark shades homing a few birds.

Beyond is the orchard, and down its avenues of mould-smitten trees the path leads to the paddocks, with their mushrooms and fairy-rings, and to the flatlands that stretch to the girding hills.

2

The farm is distant from the high-road
half a mile.

The child of the farm
does not realize it for several years.
He wanders through the orchard
finds mushrooms in the paddock
or beetles in the pond.

But one day he goes to the high-road,
sees carts and carriages pass
and men go marketing.

A traction engine crashes into his vision
with flame and smoke
and makes his eager soul retreat.

He turns away:
The huntsmen are galloping over the fields,
their red coats and the swift whimpering hounds.

XII. ON THE HEATH

White humours veining Earth
the lymphic winds of Spring
veil an early morning
when on the hill
men in cool sleeves dig the soil,
turning the loam or acrid manure
with forks that clink on stones.

Silently horses speed on the sandy track.

Lithe in white sweaters
two runners lean against a fountain.

XIII. GARDEN PARTY

I have assumed a conscious sociability,
pressed unresponding hands,
sipped tea,
and chattered aimlessly
all afternoon,

Achieving spontaneity
only
when my eyes lit at the sight
of a scarlet spider
running over the bright
green mould of an apple-tree.

XIV. CONCERT PARTY

That white hand poised
above the ivory keys
will soon descend to
shatter
the equable surface of my reverie.

To what abortion
will the silence give birth?

Noon of moist heat and the moan
of raping bees
and light like a sluice of molten gold
on the satiate petitioning leaves.

In yellow fields
mute agony of reapers.

Does the metallic horizon
give release?

Yes: higher,
    against the wider void the immaculate
    angels of lust
Lean
    on the swanbreasts of heaven.

XV. CHAMP DE MANŒUVRES

This hill indents my soul
so that I sag
like a silver mist about its flanks.

I dwell
in the golden setting of the sun
while on the plain
the illumin'd mists invade
leaf-burden'd trees.

And then
the silent tides of melting light
assail the hill, imbue
my errant soul.

The empty body broods
one with the inanimate rocks.

The last rays are fierce and irritant.
Then on the lonely hill my body wakes
and gathers to its shell my startled soul.

XVI. MOVEMENT OF TROOPS

We entrain in open trucks
and soon glide away
    from the plains of Artois.

With a wake of white smoke
we plunge
down dark avenues of silent trees.

A watcher sees
our red light gleam
occasionally.

XVII. WINTER GRIEF

Life so brief . . .
    Yet I am old
        with an era of grief.

The earth unveils
    a sad nakedness
And her hills
    droop round my sorrow.
Into the stillness
    living things scream
and only the nerveless dead
    get tranquillity.
From the funereal mould
late asters blaspheme.

XVIII. PROMENADE SOLENNELLE

We walked mutely
    over black moors
    where gray walls crawl
Sinuously into still horizons.

I was mute—
    a sticky bud
    only to unfurl
in the germination of your mood.

But you called gray rain
    to slake my heart:
you called gray mist
    over the black moors.

We passed black altars of rock:
two mute processional docile Christs
amid the unheeding
bleakness.

23

XIX. THE SORROWS OF UNICUME

1

Fresh in the flush light gleam
the slape new furrows:
ride the clean horizon rib
lithe Unicume and his roan team.

Man moulded with Earth—
like clay uprisen:
his whistling mingles
with the throstle's this even.

Inward from furtive woods
the stretched light stains:
end-toil star now broods
deeming resthaven due.

Unyoked the roan team
garthward he leads:
hooves beat to harness clink;
the swollen sun bleeds.

2

When alone Unicume
seeks his darkening dale.
Yon my white garden-rail—
Heart's tomb within!

He lifts latch to the quiet room
where yet it seems she breathes:
he kneels to take her stark hands
in caress mute with the gloom.

'*Draw the casement; let me see*
last light without.'
Ah, fierce the white white stars to hurt,
their beauty a wild shout.

Retch of flower scent, lush decay
among time-burdened shrubs.
And near and shallowly buried lay
love once enflesh'd, now fled.

3

Harsh my heart is,
scalded with grief:
my life a limp
worm-eaten leaf.

White flower unfeeling,
you star the mould:
evolvèd calmness,
my heart enfold.

XX. NIGHT

The dark steep roofs chisel
The infinity of the sky:

But the white moonlit gables
Resemble
Still hands at prayer.

NAKED WARRIORS
(1919)

PARODY OF A FORGOTTEN BEAUTY

War through my soul has driven
Its jagged blades :
The riven
Dream fades—
So you'd better grieve, heart, in the gathering night,
Grieve, heart, in the loud twilight.

KNEESHAW GOES TO WAR

Reule thyself, that other folk may rede
And trouthe shall delivere, it is no drede.
                                        CHAUCER

I

Ernest Kneeshaw grew
In the forest of his dreams
Like a woodland flower whose anæmic petals
Need the sun.

Life was a far perspective
Of high black columns
Flanking, arching and encircling him.
He never, even vaguely, tried to pierce
The gloom about him,
But was content to contemplate
His finger-nails and wrinkled boots.

He might at least have perceived
A sexual atmosphere;
But even when his body burned and urged
Like the buds and roots around him,
Abash'd by the will-less promptings of his flesh,
He continued to contemplate his feet.

2

Kneeshaw went to war.
On bleak moors and among harsh fellows
They set about with much painstaking
To straighten his drooping back:

But still his mind reflected things
Like a cold steel mirror—emotionless;
Yet in reflecting he became accomplish'd
And, to some extent,
Divested of ancestral gloom.
Then Kneeshaw crossed the sea.

At Boulogne
He cast a backward glance across the harbours
And saw there a forest of assembled masts and rigging.
Like the sweep from a releas'd dam,
His thoughts flooded unfamiliar paths:

This forest was congregated
From various climates and strange seas:
Hadn't each ship some separate memory
Of sunlit scenes or arduous waters?
Didn't each bring in the high glamour
Of conquering force?
Wasn't the forest-gloom of their assembly
A body built of living cells,
Of personalities and experiences
—A witness of heroism
Co-existent with man?

And that dark forest of his youth—
Couldn't he liberate the black columns
Flanking, arching, encircling him with dread?
Couldn't he let them spread from his vision like a fleet
Taking the open sea,
Disintegrating into light and colour and the fragrance of winds?
And perhaps in some thought they would return
Laden with strange merchandise—
And with the passing thought
Pass unregretted into far horizons.

These were Kneeshaw's musings
Whilst he yet dwelt in the romantic fringes.

3

Then, with many other men,
He was transported in a cattle-truck
To the scene of war.

30

For a while chance was kind
Save for an inevitable
Searing of the mind.
But later Kneeshaw's war
Became intense.
The ghastly desolation
Sank into men's hearts and turned them black—
Cankered them with horror.
Kneeshaw felt himself
A cog in some great evil engine,
Unwilling, but revolv'd tempestuously
By unseen springs.
He plunged with listless mind
Into the black horror.

4

There are a few left who will find it hard to forget
Polygonveld.
The earth was scarr'd and broken
By torrents of plunging shells;
Then wash'd and sodden with autumnal rains.
And Polygonbeke
(Perhaps a rippling stream
In the days of Kneeshaw's gloom)
Spread itself like a fatal quicksand,—
A sucking, clutching death.
They had to be across the beke
And in their line before dawn.
A man who was marching by Kneeshaw's side
Hesitated in the middle of the mud,
And slowly sank, weighted down by equipment and arms.
He cried for help;
Rifles were stretched to him;
He clutched and they tugged,
But slowly he sank.
His terror grew—
Grew visibly when the viscous ooze
Reached his neck.

And there he seemed to stick,
Sinking no more.
They could not dig him out—
The oozing mud would flow back again.

The dawn was very near.

An officer shot him through the head:
Not a neat job—the revolver
Was too close.

5

Then the dawn came, silver on the wet brown earth.

Kneeshaw found himself in the second wave:
The unseen springs revolved the cog
Through all the mutations of that storm of death.
He started when he heard them cry 'Dig in!'
He had to think and couldn't for a while.
Then he seized a pick from the nearest man
And clawed passionately upon the churned earth.
With satisfaction his pick
Cleft the skull of a buried man.
Kneeshaw tugged the clinging pick,
Saw its burden and shrieked.

For a second or two he was impotent
Vainly trying to recover his will, but his senses prevailing.

Then mercifully
A hot blast and riotous detonation
Hurled his mangled body
Into the beautiful peace of coma.

6

There came a day when Kneeshaw,
Minus a leg, on crutches,

Stalked the woods and hills of his native land.
And on the hills he would sing this war-song:

The forest gloom breaks:
The wild black masts
Seaward sweep on adventurous ways:
I grip my crutches and keep
A lonely view.

I stand on this hill and accept
The pleasure my flesh dictates
I count not kisses nor take
Too serious a view of tobacco.

Judas no doubt was right
In a mental sort of way:
For he betrayed another and so
With purpose was self-justified.
But I delivered my body to fear—
I was a bloodier fool than he.

I stand on this hill and accept
The flowers at my feet and the deep
Beauty of the still tarn;
Chance that gave me a crutch and a view
Gave me these.

The soul is not a dogmatic affair
Like manliness, colour, and light;
But these essentials there be:
To speak truth and so rule oneself
That other folk may rede.

The Scene of War

And perhaps some outer horror,
some hideousness to stamp beauty
a mark
on our hearts.

H.D.

I. VILLAGES DÉMOLIS

The villages are strewn
in red and yellow heaps of rubble:

Here and there
interior walls
lie upturned and interrogate the skies amazedly.

Walls that once held
within their cubic confines
a soul that now lies strewn
in red and yellow
heaps of rubble.

II. THE CRUCIFIX

His body is smashed
through the belly and chest
the head hangs lopsided
from one nail'd hand.

Emblem of agony
we have smashed you!

III. FEAR

Fear is a wave
beating through the air
and on taut nerves impinging
till there it wins
vibrating chords.

All goes well
so long as you tune the instrument
to simulate composure.

(So you will become
a gallant gentleman.)

But when the strings are broken
then you will grovel on the earth
and your rabbit eyes
will fill with the fragments of your shatter'd soul.

IV. THE HAPPY WARRIOR

His wild heart beats with painful sobs
his strain'd hands clench an ice-cold rifle
his aching jaws grip a hot parch'd tongue
his wide eyes search unconsciously.

He cannot shriek.

Bloody saliva
dribbles down his shapeless jacket.

I saw him stab
and stab again
a well-killed Boche.

This is the happy warrior,
this is he. . . .

V. LIEDHOLZ

When I captured Liedholz
I had a blacken'd face
like a nigger's
and my teeth like white mosaics shone.

We met in the night at half-past one
between the lines.
Liedholz shot at me
and I at him;
in the ensuing tumult he surrendered to me.

Before we reached our wire
he told me he had a wife and three children.
In the dug-out we gave him a whiskey.
Going to the Brigade with my prisoner at dawn
the early sun made the land delightful
and larks rose singing from the plain.

In broken French we discussed
Beethoven, Nietzsche and the International.

He was a professor
Living at Spandau
and not too intelligible.

But my black face and nigger's teeth
amused him.

VI. THE REFUGEES

Mute figures with bowed heads
They travel along the road:
Old women, incredibly old
and a hand-cart of chattels.

They do not weep:
their eyes are too raw for tears.

Past them have hastened
processions of retreating gunteams
baggage-wagons and swift horsemen.
Now they struggle along
with the rearguard of a broken army.

We shall hold the enemy towards nightfall
and they will move
mutely into the dark behind us,
only the creaking cart
disturbing their sorrowful serenity.

VII. MY COMPANY

*Foule! Ton âme entière est debout
dans mon corps.*
                              JULES ROMAINS

I

You became
in many acts and quiet observances
a body and a soul, entire.

I cannot tell
what time your life became mine:
perhaps when one summer night

37

we halted on the roadside
in the starlight only
and you sang your sad home-songs
dirges which I standing outside you
coldly condemned.

Perhaps, one night, descending cold
when rum was mighty acceptable
and my doling gave birth to sensual gratitude.

And then our fights: we've fought together
compact, unanimous
and I have felt the pride of leadership.

In many acts and quiet observances
you absorbed me:
Until one day I stood eminent
and I saw you gather'd round me
uplooking
and about you a radiance that seemed to beat
with variant glow and to give
grace to our unity.

But, God! I know that I'll stand
someday in the loneliest wilderness
someday my heart will cry
for the soul that has been, but that now
is scatter'd with the winds,
deceased and devoid.

I know that I'll wander with a cry:
'O beautiful men, O men I loved
O whither are you gone, my company?'

2

My men go wearily
with their monstrous burdens.
They bear wooden planks
and iron sheeting
through the area of death.

When a flare curves through the sky
they rest immobile.

Then on again
Sweating and blaspheming—
'Oh, bloody Christ!'

My men, my modern Christs
your bloody agony confronts the world.

3

A man of mine
    lies on the wire.
It is death to fetch his soulless corpse.

A man of mine
    lies on the wire;
And he will rot
and first his lips
the worms will eat.
It is not thus I would have him kiss'd
but with the warm passionate lips
of his comrade here.

4

I can assume
a giant attitude and godlike mood
and then detachedly regard
all riots, conflicts and collisions.

The men I've lived with
lurch suddenly into a far perspective:
They distantly gather like a dark cloud of birds
in the autumn sky.

Urged by some unanimous
volition or fate
Clouds clash in opposition:
The sky quivers, the dead descend;
earth yawns.

They are all of one species.

From my giant attitude
in godlike mood
I laugh till space is filled
with hellish merriment.

Then again I assume
my human docility
bow my head
and share their doom.

VIII. THE EXECUTION OF
CORNELIUS VANE

*Le combat spirituel est aussi brutal que la
bataille d'hommes; mais la vision de la
justice est le plaisir de Dieu seul.*

ARTHUR RIMBAUD

Arraign'd before his worldly gods
He would have said:
'I, Cornelius Vane,
A fly in the sticky web of life,
Shot away my right index finger.

I was alone, on sentry, in the chill twilight after dawn,
And the act cost me a bloody sweat.
Otherwise the cost was trivial—they had no evidence.
And I lied to the wooden fools who tried me.
When I returned from hospital
They made me a company cook:
I peel potatoes and other men fight.'

For nearly a year Cornelius peeled potatoes
And his life was full of serenity.
Then the enemy broke our line
And their hosts spread over the plains
Like unleash'd beads.
Every man was taken—
Shoemakers, storemen, grooms—
And arms were given them
That they might stem the oncoming host.

Cornelius held out his fingerless hand
And remarked that he couldn't shoot.
'But you can stab,' the sergeant said,
So he fell in with the rest, and, a little group,
They marched away towards the enemy.

After an hour they halted for a rest.
They were already in the fringe of the fight:
Desultory shells fell about them,
And past them retreating gunteams
Galloped in haste.
But they must go on.

Wounded stragglers came down the road,
Haggard and limping
Their arms and equipment tossed away.
Cornelius Vane saw them, and his heart was beating wildly,
For he must go on.

41

At the next halt
He went aside to piss,
And whilst away a black shell
Burst near him:
Hot metal shrieked past his face;
Bricks and earth descended like hail,
And the acrid stench of explosive filled his nostrils.

Cornelius pitched his body to the ground
And crouched in trembling fear.
Another shell came singing overhead,
Nowhere near.

But Cornelius sprang to his feet, his pale face set.
He willed nothing, saw nothing, only before him
Were the free open fields:
To the fields he ran.

He was still running when he began to perceive
The tranquillity of the fields
And the battle distant.
Away in the north-east were men marching on a road;
Behind were the smoke-puffs of shrapnel,
And in the west the sun declining
In a sky of limpid gold.

When night came finally
He had reached a wood.
In the thickness of the trees
The cold wind was excluded,
And here he slept a few hours.

In the early dawn
The chill mist and heavy dew
Pierced his bones and wakened him.
There was no sound of battle to be heard.

In the open fields again
The sun shone sickly through the mist
And the dew was icy to the feet.
So Cornelius ran about in that white night,
The sun's wan glare his only guide.

Coming to a canal
He ran up and down like a dog
Deliberating where to cross.
One way he saw a bridge
Loom vaguely, but approaching
He heard voices and turned about.
He went far the other way,
But growing tired before he found a crossing,
Plunged into the icy water and swam.
The water gripped with agony;
His clothes sucked the heavy water,
And as he ran again
Water oozed and squelched from his boots
His coat dripped and his teeth chattered.

He came to a farm.
Approaching cautiously, he found it deserted.
Within he discarded his sopping uniform, dried himself and
    donned
Mufti he found in a cupboard.
Dark mouldy bread and bottled cider he also found
And was refreshed.
Whilst he was eating,
Suddenly,
Machine-guns opened fire not far away,
And their harsh throbbing
Darkened his soul with fear.

The sun was more golden now,
And as he went—
Always going west—
The mist grew thin.

About noon,
As he skirted the length of a wood
The warmth had triumphed and the spring day was beautiful.
Cornelius perceived with a new joy
Pale anemones and violets of the wood,
And wished that he might ever
Exist in the perception of these woodland flowers
And the shafts of yellow light that pierced
The green dusk.

Two days later
He entered a village and was arrested.
He was hungry, and the peace of the fields
Dissipated the terror that had been the strength of his will.

He was charged with desertion
And eventually tried by court-martial.

The evidence was heavy against him,
And he was mute in his own defence.
A dumb anger and a despair
Filled his soul.

He was found guilty.
Sentence: To suffer death by being shot.

The sentence duly confirmed,
One morning at dawn they led him forth.
He saw a party of his own regiment,
With rifles, looking very sad.
The morning was bright, and as they tied
The cloth over his eyes, he said to the assembly:
'What wrong have I done that I should leave these:
The bright sun rising
And the birds that sing?'

ADDITIONAL POEMS FROM THE PERIOD OF THE FIRST WORLD WAR

AEROPLANES

A dragonfly
in the flecked grey sky.

Its silvered planes
break the wide and still
harmony of space.

Around it shells
flash
their fumes
burgeoning to blooms
smoke-lilies that float
along the sky.

Among them darts
a dragonfly.

YPRES

I

With a chill and hazy light
the sun of a winter noon
swills
thy ruins.

Thy ruins etched
in silver silhouettes
against a turquoise sky.

Lank poles leap to the infinite
their broken wires
tossed like the rat-locks of Maenades.

47

And Desolation broods over all
   gathering to her lap
      her leprous children.

The sparrows whimper
   amid the broken arches.

2

Sunset
  licks the ruins
    with vermeil flames.
The flames rise and fall
   against the dusking sky—
against the dusking sky
flames fall and die.

Heaped in the black night
   are the grey ashes
     of desolation.

But even now the moon
   blooms
     like a cankered rose
and with a soft passionate light
   kisses
     the wan harmonies of ruin.

THE AUTUMN OF THE WORLD

As a host of blood-flecked clouds
　　skim the golden sky
　　　　and melt into the vermilioned vastness
there comes borne on a wind
　　from the infinite womb of chaos
　　　　the dank wafture of decay.

Over the eternal waters of the sea
　　that weep and find no solace for their cares
lethargic vultures flock and swirl
　　and fill the echoes with their gloomy songs.

Hot winds from tropic zones
　　betray
　　　　the transient things of Earth.
The last yellow leaves fall
　　on the iridescent sward.
The wind dies
　　and the Summer voices are forever still.

AUGURIES OF LIFE AND DEATH
(In memory of Charles Read, 1897-1918)

I

The autumn leaves were an augury
And seemed to intend
As they yellowly drooped in the languid air
That life was a fragile mood and death
A tremendous despair.

The yellow leaves fell
Like slow tears of gold on the face of the day:
They fell to the earth with a faint sad sigh.

D

They sighed
As the feet of the passers-by
Crushed them into the moist black soil:
They sighed when the gentle wind
Lifted them along the way.

In the park
Old men swept the dead things in a heap to burn:
Their last fragrance
Floated about the naked trees.

I thought as the women walked in the moist still day
Wearing yellow chrysanthemums in their coats
A chrysanthemum was
A pale dishevelled emblem of death.

The sun
Was a silver pervasion across the sky:
From the sky
The dead leaves fell.

2

Some well-meaning fool
called him an unconscious Sidney
proudly dying in the surge of battle.
Many said
he paid the supreme sacrifice. . . .

Let us be frank for once:
Such foisted platitudes
cannot console sick hearts.
Rather this alone is clear:
He was a delightful youth
irradiating joy, peculiarly loved
by hundreds of his fellows.
The impulse of his living
left a wake of laughter
and happiness in the hearts of sad men.

Then this glad progression
is suddenly cut short
annihilated.
We hear
he was killed in action, leading his men. . . .
In a moment that life and its radiance
went out like a blown flame.

No natural logic can explain
that harsh departure and our dark void.
The knotted bitterness grips tight
I curse the fate that sent us
a tortured species down the torrent of life
soul-exposed to insensate shores
and the dark fall of death.

Yet in the scene of life
a consolation I can find.
All things do cry
vain is rebellion.
Is not the gargoyle leer of fate
in all its impassive cruelty
known too well
for any man to rebel?
The tendrils of our intensest emotions
are torn by its inane force
and strewn in bleeding death.
But no devastation can
utterly kill:
in the burnt blackness of earth
built from invisible beginnings
womb-warmth will engender
an animate thing.

So we might make his short delightful life
an instance of those beauties that adorn
tragically the earth with flowers
heroes and valiant hearts.

This flower hold dear
till the years evolve in their callous recession
a memorized beauty.

3

All the world is wet with tears
and droops its languid life
in sympathy.
But death is beautiful with pride: the trees
are golden lances whose brave array
assails the sadness of the day.
They do not meet
fate with an angry tumult:
Serene they stay
austerely dying day by day:
Their golden lances imperceptibly fade
into the sleep of winter, their victory made
in the hearts of men.

MUTATIONS OF THE PHOENIX
(1923)

MUTATIONS OF THE PHOENIX

Beauty, truth and rarity,
Grace in all simplicity,
Here enclosed in cinders lie.

I

We have rested our limbs
   in some forsaken cove
where wide black horns of rock
Weigh on the subdued waters
   the waters
     menaced to quiet.

Our limbs
   settle into the crumbling sand.
There will be our impress here
   until the flowing tide
     erases
all designs the fretful day leaves here.

The blood burns in our limbs with an even flame.
The same sundering flame
   has burnt the world and left these crumbling sands.
The one flame
   burns many phenomena.

The limbs
   have their arcadian lethargy
holding the included flame
   to a temporal submission.

The flame
   burns all
     uses
   the ducts and chambers of our tunnelled flesh
   to focus flame
     to its innate intensity.

Flame
   is a whirl of atoms.
At one moment a whorl of what is seen—
   a shell.

A shell
   convoluted through time—
      endless and beginningless time.

Will this sea
   throw such symbols round our limbs
      when the white surf recedes?
Does a white flame
   burn among the waves?

Will a phoenix arise
   from a womb evolv'd
      among the curved crests of foam?
At Aphrodite's birth
   were the waters in white flame?

2

Why should I dwell in individual ecstasy?
It is a hollow quarry of the mind
rill'd with rock drippings, smooth'd with silt;
and only the whorlminded Hamlet walks there
musing in the gutters.

We now leave this infinite well,
where naught is found—naught is definite,
to emerge:
to scan the round of vision,
a greedy eye wanting things finite
and enumerate to the mind.

3

Mind wins deciduously,
hibernating through many years.

Impulse alone is immutable sap
and flowing continuance
extending life to leafy men.
Effort of consciousness
    carries from origin
        the metamorphic clue.
The cap is here
in conscience humanly unique;
and conscience is control, ordaining the strain
to some perfection
    not briefly known.

4

We must not be oversubtle with these fools
else we defeat ourselves, not urging them.
They are in the filmy undergrowth
driven by frenzies whom they see
seductively mirrored in their minds.
Yet how persuade a mind that the thing seen
is habitant of the cerebral cave
and has elsewhere no materiality?
    But like a lily lust
        haunting the wither'd groins of crones
    is a phantom desperate to reason.
    Shall the phoenix devour
        the horrid insurrection?
His flames are incinerary of much evil—
of all evil evident to the mind.
But here where naught but sick moonshine
is thrown from reflective facets
the seductive are the more lustreful phantoms.
In the clearings: in solar ruddiness
ends lunar moodiness.
There silhouettes are etched
    not phantomly
but in living areas of the mind.

The sea fringe breaks
along the yellow shore
and is finite to the vision.
So time breaks in spume and fret
of intersifted worlds.
Our world is invisible
   till vision
      makes a finite reflection.
Then the world is finite—
   cast in the mould and measure
      of a finite instrument.

You can't escape: don't escape
poor easeless human mind.
Better leave things finite.
See where that curl'd surf clashes
in a wreath, in a running crest,
   in a fan of white flame!
All the past lives there—
   lives as time breaks
      in spume and fret of intersifted worlds.

All existence
   past, present and to be
      is in this sea fringe.
There is no other temporal scene.

6

The phoenix burns spiritually
   among the fierce stars
      and in the docile brain's recesses.
Its ultimate spark
you cannot trace.
Its spark out
and out is existence.
Time ends: time being vision—
reflected interaction of any elements.

But vision is fire.
Light burns the world in the focus of an eye.
The eye is all: is hierarch of the finite world.
Eye gone light gone, and the unknown is very near.

7

Phoenix, bird of terrible pride,
ruddy eye and iron beak!
Come, leave the incinerary nest;
spread your red wings

And soaring in the golden light
survey the world;
hover against the highest sky;
menace men with your strange phenomena.

For a haunt seek a coign
in a rocky land;
when the night is black
settle on the bleak headlands.

Utter shrill warnings in the cold dawn sky;
let them descend
into the shutter'd minds below you.
Inhabit our wither'd nerves.

8

This is the holy phoenix time.
The sun is sunken in a deep abyss
her dying life transpires.

Each bar and boss
of rallied cloud the fire receives.

Till the ashen sky dissolves.

The mind seeks ease
      now that the moon has risen
            and the world itself is full of ease.

The embers of the world
      rustle, fall: a bird's wing, a dry leaf.
There is a faint glow of embers
      in the ashen sky.

These stars
      are your final ecstasy,
and the moon now risen
      golden, easeful.

The hills creep in mistily—
      the tide now a distant sigh—
like hounds outstretched
they guard the included peace—
      the tide a muted ecstasy.

The river carries in its slaty bed
      an echo from the sea.

But we leave
      even the river is lost.

No sound now.
No colour: all black: a cave.

In the cavern's mouth
the moon is hidden.

Yet still the stars—
      intense remnants of time.

O phoenix,
O merciful bird of fire,
Extinguish your white
      hungry flames.

JOHN DONNE DECLINES A BENEFICE

'. . . You know, Sir, who says 'Happy is that man whose con-
science does not accuse him for that thing which he does.' To these
I might add other reasons that dissuade me; but I crave your favour
that I might forbear to express them, and thankfully decline your offer.'

Walton's Life of Dr Donne

Shut out the sound.—These June birds shrill
Their easy ecstasies too well
To make a music for the thoughts
That deep within discordantly delve
This fallow mind. Now seal
The circling conscience in a whiten'd wall
Of calm decision. So reach the still
Mental height where Time will bring
A naked peace—the while an avid throng
Hustles in the dim sunken gulf.

There only this remains: to be a self
Determined by the building brain—
The mind in a heaven attained alone.
Sects climb by fallible stairs
And ways unlit by thinking eyes.
The ego sings an individual praise,
Graceful enough to God—whose mind is mine;
Who is this supple flesh and bone
Aggrandised in aeriness, eaten by no worms
Of dutiful doubt. No alarms
Fret that lonely omnipotence;
He is one and has none higher to enhance
Enormously the wavering needle of a will.
But he to man is a magnetic North, a call
For conscience to settle toward,
And through the tossings of a stormy run
Rest as quiescent as it can
Till it attain its set attraction in death.
Then there's extinction—good enough, in all truth

To dissolve in its dark motionless vat
The heart's stony clot
Of fast fermented flesh.
Would that the will set there! What a hush
There would be in the individual earth,
And a calm setting-forth
To meet Christ or Satan with an apposite jest.
But no: death is a blast
To exclude with woollens if wonder's wan.
If you live lustily you bare the skin,
Take chance in sinew'd arms
And cloth'd in energies scorn stabbing storms
Till finally they fell you and derisively heap
Over your bones boulders of faith and hope.

Yet what of the molten soul in that labyrinth?
Meet we men there contained in shells
Of throughshine flesh, a tenth
As corporeal as skinless skulls?
But yet persons of dower'd import,
Hailing each other in that sphere
Beyond earth, water, air and fire—
Souls that leave their bodies and depart
And rise like corks to the outer rim
Where elements cease and the gloom
Of matter is consumed in the glare
Of a timeless radiance, an intangible fire
That does not stain those white souls black
As Æthiops engender'd under a lusty sun,
But gloriously transmutes their earthly sin.
This is a garden where souls do find
Spiritual limbs and genitals.
Yet doubt dissembles all—there's aid
In equilibrium alone,
Holding the middle plane
Like Mahmed in his shroud and leaden sheet.
The mind can uproot
The earth these numb feet stand upon

And make it spin about the sun.
Thus is the symmetry of God's world destroy'd
To make a logic on a scroll.
What folly's there—to reflect
On perfect mirrors the imperfect all!
Think how the lovely is lost in the act!
Once I was Jack Donne, burned by the vast
Energies of an eager lust,
And leapt with zeal
Into the mirage of a limpid pool
Which my impinging body crackt
Into a crater, a sulphurous hole
Of faithless lechery.
I reattained the fresh atmospheres
By the perfection of a fair fantasy,
This heart's concern, a sun to shine
In the night of lust.

     So shall the soul invade
The world of the imaginary divine
In which the fanatic can abandon selfhood.
But a sick pride calls the act profane—
To rid this soul of its compact kingdom
And give it a crystal nothingness,
The body left, a wickless mass
Of inchoation. There's some divine amalgam
Of flesh and spirit, an alloy
Which I must find—must make my God
Invisibly from spit and clay.

But Oh! that skill might achieve some end:
Make choice and be! My breast,
Heavy as a thundercloud, longs for impact
And sonorous riot, tassell'd with light
Of mortal power. Now Morton takes my hand
And all too impressively points a way
For this mind amorous of conflict. And there's action
   there—

Men to be moved by brighter shine than Satan's lure!
This circled breast could burst its load
Of clamorous appeal till the wingéd angels heed
The message and its personal seal.
My sheaf of snakes I'll turn to whips
Of merciless castigation. And cups
Of solace then I'll pour
On every pulver'd spreading scar.
My mind will move
In alternate circles of hate and love . . .

If the propulsion for such scheme
Were generate in this complex frame!
Come, give it comprest thought,
End this fever of muscles distraught.
Sit. Relax these legs and arms,
Even to the digit tips. A racked heretic squirms
Scarce more remarkably. So. Now hangs my soul
In compos'd aeriness. The tempests fall
To yellow calm . . .

        There's Paracelsus' craft
Wherein man can be expressed
In dying monuments . . . My fancy lingers there
Only a while, to endure
A last defeat. I have learning in the law,
And, practised in a soft tongue and genteel bow,
Might give my spirit ease in worldly power.
But there's subservience to one in whom
Dalliance lives—who could for a whim
Debase my structure ere I'd done.

What remains? Aver Casaubon's light?
The Annals of Baronius refute?
Conjure with Mirandula's name?
Or from Sebonde select a theme?
There's food enough for wit
In this present service. With it,

And leave and leisure to elaborate my thought,
I'd be content. The soul, enlarged in solitude,
Diminishes to naught the vain parade
That buttresses on empty pates.

But there's no guarantee: Morton departs
And I am outcast in a wrangling world
Where an evolvéd soul's of no avail,
Save for the delight of wits. And I scorn
To pour out my soul to their flatten'd gaze—
Its craft is my own, secretly to devise.

Budded emotions swell and show green sheaths
Piercing to their wanted light.
From these I must gently cultivate
Ingenious trees, threading their laths
Of leaves and twigs into the air of heaven.
Such monuments will wane
Many men's lives; or even
Petrify to indestructible stone.
To build such monuments is the test
Of life's worth to the will: to fail
Is to burn flesh and spirit in the fast
Flames of the dissolute self—
To acknowledge this vessel an empty drum
Beaten by chance; and vision the whim
Of heated brains. Thus is hell entail'd.
I must complete the dizzy tower;
Rectify Babel's shame and Job's despair,
And in the fullness of one made all
Pour this hydroptic flesh and aery soul,
Death emptying the vessel quite.

But chaunt prayers, mechanically shrive
Melancholy sinners fearful of their fate?
Vent manhood in a carping rave
Against the hoofed devil? Fade into age

Full of dissembling sanctity, a palsied doge
His city built into the sea of lust
On rotting piles? Youth a smirk
Of unleashed thought . . . Memory a blast
With'ring my grey hairs . . . I'll not! I'll not!
Quick! To Morton! The will is set!

THE RETREAT

When in some sudden hush of earth
The pulsing rhythm is lost, and I am alone
With all those melancholy forces of the mind
That wait for empty moments, with no sound
Of living things, or vocal throats, or any of the subtle
Crepitations that betray
The sense in things—when in some sudden hush
I fall a victim to the ghouls
I buried years ago in a sepulchre
Of calm amnesia, then once more
I see the screen the years have built
Between this day and the patterns wrought
In love and battle by the ecstatic heart.
Again I strive
To hold the real design of life
Within the intenser
Light of the mind in these moments. I cannot tell
If this calm be illusion; or if
The fiendish days were real.
I know that then I lived
Like the clean movement of a wheel
Flying on so fair an axle that the eye
Can hardly make its motion. The mind was absent then
Or but a mirror, passively receiving
The body's ritual—a body that would glide
On quivering wings, against the sun,

And never note
The world that lay beneath, pensive with agony.
But now, the world is real and calm:
The body lives, a limp container
Of this bounding mind;
And the mind notes the visible world—
How it moves with mechanic evenness,
Dismissing hope and hasty exaltations.
The mind is melancholy, and frets
On all the futile longingness of men,
Their fantasies and thought-selected dreams.
I hold a little to the living earth,
Now so quiescent;
I hold no less to that mental life
I would at least in fancy
Mingle with the base of things—
Not mind and matter, co-distinct
In man alone, or alone in living things,
But a tympanum for the rhythms of ether,
An element
Incarnate in everything. Life is but a lesser lesion
Of this extensive energy, and so life is less
A thing to wonder at and worship—
Is but one mechanism more to manifest the force
Active even in the gulfs of uncreated space.

So let these agonies, wrung from the utterly fragile
Frame of human life, be at rest,
Perspectively doomed and wrought
To the little loudness of an insect's cry.
What matter now
The mind's phantom inquisitors?
What if they unleash the blood-loving hounds
And all the unlimited woes of hate?
These echo faintly in the corridors
Carved cavernously wherever the mind
Looks down into the waste of stars.

Liberty and power, and that light-winged joy
That is the folly of forgetfulness,
These do not come in the unguarded
Moods of quiet. At that time
The unhealing features of the brain
Revive their dim wounds, to burn, to bleed,
To flow with the lava of thought's lucid pain.

Oh, turn your milk-dim eyes
To outer things! See where a haze
Trembles against the hard horizon,
Quivering in a rhythm that calls to mind
The ultimate harmony of the world!
The same rhythm
Governs the structure of all that's seen
And felt and heard—of all that's known
In the deep percipient heart of man.
This mind alone, like a rock
Rebounding disharmoniously down some precipice
Is carried by unconscious force
Till death give it inertia.

But the same mind has seen
Beauties beyond its reach, perfections
Never to be attain'd. Some state of high serenity
Exists beyond the range
Of fever'd sense.
The starv'd heart sickens
In longingness, and from this sickness
Emerges the troubled drift of men. The past,
Now like a riot of dreamy horror,
Is this heart's sickness, and its diurnal function.

The still day; a river at my feet;
And the yellow leaf that flags
In the calm cincture of the hollow'd bank—
These and all percipient joys,
These are the dreamland state.

We wake to conflict: the mind is in a prison
With a high small window, barr'd against escape.
A decoy of light enters there,
Reminding the tortur'd brain that somewhere unseen
The wide perfection of the sun's way exists.
Beyond time and space there is a beauty
Not to be seized by men in prison, who but languish
In shackles carried from the womb, and worn
Unto the release of death: unto the dark return
Of the world's harmony.

THE ANALYSIS OF LOVE

Else a great Prince in prison lies.
JOHN DONNE

1

I would have my own vision
     The world's vision:
The beauty settled in my mind
     A lamp in a busy street.

Yet these activities are too intimate,
     Made for a solitary sense:
However builded the emotion
     The imagination's mute.

Could voice join mind's eye and scream
     Its vision out
Then the world would halt its toil
     Passionless, time unreal.

2

I see black branches bend
     In leafy towers;
For trees like men have skeletons
     And temporal bodies of green flesh.

69

My capillaries disperse
    A dense foliage of cells.
She enters my red shade like a woodpecker
    Fluttering against me with spread wings.

Up and down my galled trunk
    She travels with a petulant bill
And satiate sings
    In the moist shadow of my intricate heart.

3

Night palliates
    The ragged ridge of things;
The stars, however minute, are intense
    And pierce beyond the reckoning brain.

The stars and the dark palliation
    Are not indwelling
When driven lust has dark dominion
    In the mind's eclipse.

Yet sleep is relentless, extinguishing all
    Under its cone of annihilation;
And in the fresh and cool morning
    The lusting man is lost.

4

And lust is a finite thing
    Deftly to be sized by the passionless mind
Lust gone, other elements exist
    Wrought in the body's being.

The measuring mind can appraise
    An earthen grace;
The idiot's chatter
    Analyses into experience.

But your appeal is imperceptible
  As ultimate atoms
And the fast matrix
  Of all within the human universe.

5

In vain I have searched the visible earth
  For any symbol of our love:
Doves, elephants and Abelards
  Have seemed too empty of our mood.

They are too finite in their wooing
  Linked by ambitious bonds:
I court you in the commonplace
  And a wonder is in our path.

Rather we are like a plant's cells
  Invisibly one;
Or the silicious crystal built
  When the heart of a mountain cools.

6

There are moments when I see your mind
  Laps'd in your sex;
When one particular deployment
  Is the reflex of incomplete attainment.

These moments vanish
  Like lamps at daybreak:
The wide and even light
  Is kind and real.

And then you are universal;
  I too: our minds,
Not cramp'd by figured thought
  Unite in the impersonal beauty we possess.

Since you are finite you will never find
   The hidden source of the mind's emotion;
It is a pool, secret in dusk and dawn,
   Deep in the chartless forest life has grown.

Since you are blind you do not see
   The thirsting beasts peer from gnarled roots
And creep to the brink, at noon,
   To lap with rough tongues, rippling the burnish'd serenity.

—This mind which is collected
   From many tricklings, of dew and rain,
Of which you are the chief
   And freshest in its depths.

8

You will not drive me to the anguish of love
   By any torture of this faith,
Converting to the corrupted semblance of despair
   The still evidence of my look;

But by the triumph of those traits—
   Their multiplication to excess—
Which marks the frailties germinant
   In a mind emotion-bound.

Not that I fear your capture
   In human littlenesses;
These are drops we can absorb
   In the fount and flow of a passionless mood.

The teas'd fibrils of reason
   Weave vainly to dam
Some bank against the giant flood
   Of this emotion.

Waves' and winds' erosion
   Crumbles granitic cliffs,
Æonly obliterating
   The earth's known visage.

The multiple striving of the human race
   Wins slowly mind's conquest
Of brutal foes; or is the supreme foe
   This hope, deluding?

10

When you have totalled this life
   And got the vision complete:
When you have seen a central horror
   Blacking out the sun's gift—

Take me: englobe my soul
   And spin it on an axis;
Set about me ring'd planets
   And diverse atmospheres.

And in that world
   Lacking the imperfections of this
Live boldly, plant sapling trees
   Expecting a burden of fruit.

11

These gnarled trunks
   Represent no torture
Or maim of sentient life
   But are the evidence of unfelt endurance.

Know too that we
   As we grow old will wear
Faces grotesque with wrinkles
   Crowsfeet and sagging flesh.

73

But do not grieve that you must lose
    A supple beauty that I love:
As wind in twisted trees
    So life in you will leave appeal.

12

You will say that I am in the scheme of things
    A unit in the crumbling earth;
Trees are barren:
    Chance I'm a barren tree.

Link me with circumstances if you must
    But live to triumph all the same:
We'll be insensate when the whirl
    Of circumstance is past.

You'll not avoid the avalanche
    But parasitic on my soul
Run, beat, rebound and throb
    In world descent.

13

Nature has perpetual tears
    In drooping boughs
And everywhere inanimate death
    Is immemorial.

But I have naught that will express
    The grief I feel
When men and moods combine to show
    The end of this—

This mental ecstasy all spent
    In disuniting death
And the years that spread
    Oblivion on our zest.

BEATA L'ALMA

Beata l' alma, ove non corre tempo.
                    MICHELANGELO

I

Time ends when vision sees its lapse in
        liberty. The seven
sleepers quit their den and wild
        lament-
ations fill out voiceless bodies. Echoes only are.

You will never understand the mind's
        misanthropy, nor see
that all is foul and fit to
        screech in.
It is an eye's anarchy: men are ghoulish stumps

and the air a river of opaque
        filth. God! I cannot see
to design these stark reaches, these
        bulging
contours pressed against me in the maddening dark.

A blindman's buff and no distilling
        of song for the woeful
scenes of agony. Never
        will rest
the mind an instant in its birdlike flutterings.

Could I impress my voice on the plas-
        tic darkness, or lift an
inviolate lanthorn from
        a ship
in the storm I might have ease. But why? No
        fellows

75

would answer my hullallo, and my
             lanthorn would lurch on the
        mast till it dipped under the
                  wet waves
and the hissing darkness healed the wide wound of
        light.

A cynic race—to bleak ecstasies
        we are driven by our
    sombre destiny. Men's shouts
             are not
glad enough to echo in our groin'd hearts. We know

war and its dead, and famine's bleach'd bones;
             black rot overreaching
        the silent pressure of life
             in fronds
of green ferns and in the fragile shell of white flesh.

2

New children must be born of gods in
        a deathless land, where the
    uneroded rocks bound clear
             from cool
glassy tarns, and no flaw is in mind or flesh.

Sense and image they must refashion—
             they will not recreate
        love: love ends in hate; they will
             not use
words: words lie. The structure of events alone is

comprehensible and to single
             perceptions communic-
        ation is not essential.
             Art ends;
the individual world alone is valid

76

and that gives ease. The water is still;
    the rocks are hard and vein'd,
   metalliferous, yielding
     an ore
of high worth. In the sky the unsullied sun lake.

Three Shorter Poems

*

THE FALCON AND THE DOVE

I

This high-caught hooded Reason broods upon my wrist,
Fetter'd by a so tenuous leash of steel.
We are bound for the myrtle marshes, many leagues away,
And have a fair expectation of quarry.

2

Over the laggard dove, inclining to green boscage
Hovers this intentional doom—till the unsullied sky receives
A precipitation of shed feathers
And the swifter fall of wounded wings.

3

Will the plain aye echo with that loud *hullallo!*
Or retain an impress of our passage?
We have caught Beauty in a wild foray
And now the falcon is hooded and comforted away.

EQUATION

$$a + b + c = x$$

a

Hylas, the world's perceptual scene,
And man no less, the axle beam
Of mobile sense, exist but as
A notion in the mind of God.

b

And Columbine contributed,
Uttering a wise complaint:
Pierrot upon my stressèd breast—
The old moon in the new moon's arms.

c

The subtle fury of a winter dusk;
A chord dissolving in the brain—
All knowledge and ideality
Are borne in the lapse of the menstrual sea.

x

Earth is machine and works to plan,
Winnowing space and time;
The ethic mind is engine too,
Accelerating in the void.

FORMAL INCANTATION

O watery sun decline
Defame the obdurate day
Or the ashen slaves of Phoebus
Will find me with a golden key

And bid me unlock the casket laid
Beneath the crumbling stairs
Where Jason's fleece awaits the day
Medea's art recurs.

The pianola's notes resound
Through the damp rain-sodden rooms
And I have naught I can repress
Against the anguish of the herbal flames

That flicker in the near zone
Of Hecate's naked plight.
O triune grace, I will not miss
Thee at the closure of night.

COLLECTED POEMS 1913-25

(1926)

F

THE LAMENT OF SAINT DENIS

'. . . *The famous Grecian fanatic, who gave himself out for Dionysius the Areopagite, disciple of St Paul, and who, under the protection of this venerable name, gave laws and instructions to those that were desirous of raising their souls above all human things, in order to unite them to their great source by sublime contemplation . . .*'

From the Institutes of Johann Lorenz von Mosheim, translated by Archibald Maclaine (1764).

1

I, said the moon, who have been a maiden
   worshipp'd of man
am now but a burnish'd emblem
   of the sun's span.

But the old witch in me yet
   is wooing, wooing.
And mine is the light of day
   in this memorial noon.

2

O hallowed is the moon and holy
A bowl of languish'd fire. The years are cold
Seventy since the sun shone in midnight ecstasy
Seventy and each year shortening towards the noon
And then leaving this everlasting night
With a fitful symbol in the broken sky.

3

The path is steep
Narrowing between rock walls: an uncapp'd cavern
Where the ledges drip and the anguish'd winds
Woo hollows of eternal woe.
And there a rheumy host of men
Climb burden'd, stumbling in the dark unless

The clouds are torn to let the light
Stray raggedly across the land. Straining thongs
Cut their breasts: breasts will break
And spill their bloody treasure on the rocks
But still the unbroken with their burdens will climb
Between the sheer limits of stone
Into the tempest that gathers
Like a dark crown above the hill.

4

Their lips
Are held in the tension of lust, and lines
Of unenlighten'd care have cut
Across the mask upon the bone: the bone is fair in man
Only the flesh is false, puckering at the influx of light
In lewd habitual knots of vice.

5

The bones that dance after death
        are very feat, very nice
And the empty box has forgotten
        its load of rocking dice.

6

They have gathered on their backs
Arranged burdens: seventy years
Have sorted out a neat set
Of necessary tools: food for a long march
A blanket for the night, and a burden of unessential things.
All coming to a sea-level, having met there
And having a common journey to make,
They have formed into ranks
With a leader at their head.

7

At the summit there will be light, or sleep—
At least some release.

But when the sense of labour in limbs had slackened
And they were aware in the dark of a level
And of a bare reach into the sky,
They were still burdened, and in doubt
Whether to descend or wait for a dawn.

But a dawn might be very long
After the slow declension of light.

8

And then a faint rumour in the night
An approaching murmur of enemies.
Their hearts were suddenly loud in their still bodies
Fluttering wildly within those livid tunicles of flesh.

No radiance of the moon
Came to illustrate their madness,
Only the wind
To incorporate their anguish.

The menace grew louder
And out of the valley rising
Into the night came another host
Clothed in light, with limbs unveiled and free.

Their wan bodies
Contained their light;
No radiance was shed
On rocks or on the opposèd throng.

With whirlpool eyes that were innocent
They searched the night,
Eager to find for their intense thoughts
An habitation in light.

9

When they came into the presence of the silent standing men
When their guiding fingers that should meet wet rocks

Touched warm flesh,
They halted.
And out of the place where they had expected light
Out of the dark well of night
Came the tired voice of an old man:

We hold the way: no other host can pass
Save across our broken limbs, our broken breasts.
We have toiled too long: we can entertain no guest
Save death—death who will deliver us to sleep and rest.

The voice mingled with the wind shrilling in the rocks
And rippled across a bent harvest
Of mute appealing hands.

And then the wind fell to fury.
Vacuous chaos sucked air, spewed the waters of the broken
    cloud
Against flesh and stone.
The old men cowered under the rocks
Waiting for the end.

But the naked children fled together in their fear.
Too many terrors dwelt in the unseen world.
Inward, in the circle of linked arms,
They could imagine calm.

10

Out of the storm came a figure carrying its sever'd head
Like a lantern in one hand
And stood between the throngs
And waited till the wind had lost
Its melancholy eloquence, and the dark crown of clouds
Had drifted into the pervious earth.

Then on the distraught scene
The stars and the moon shed a fabulous light
And the head began to speak

Its eyes were covered with deathly lids
And the lips that moved
Were like pale rubber valves
Distended by a wayward pulse.

II

Think not that I am a storm-quelling spirit
And drive before me all the unorder'd forces of nature.
Rather I am the storm, which, sunk in me
For a while evades your senses.
I was of the lambs of the sacred flock
And honour'd for my death.
But now with a doleful symbol
I come to embody this moment of time.

On this mountain top
I stand where a dark stream of old men
Has met an impediment of light—
A dawn breaking on the southern side
Against the blue northern night.
These old men who have come to meet me here
Are sons of old men, and of old men before,
The living point of all the dark forces of the past.

And these children of light
Are the empty forms winding down to earth
There to receive sight
And objects to their senses.
These two streams cross in me,
Past and future are but two lines
Intersecting at a point: in me.
From this point of time I survey eternity
I am master of all nature and knowledge
And all that exists in time
Moves through me: these fair children
Pass into life, these old bones disintegrate.
And I, in a moment of time,
Include them all;

87

Yesterday, tomorrow, and today
Are in my single glance
And the embrace of my wither'd arms.
And here in me is the grace of living:
Many changes must I undergo
As these streams give and take
The lanterns of a temporal light.

I am chaos and dark nothingness;
The storm you met on the way
Is now held in me.
In this lightless body,
Uncrowned, ungrac'd, devoid,
The tumult reigns.
In a moment,
In any other moment,
The storm will issue,
The chaos will be without—
In the past and in the future,
Yesterday and tomorrow.

And in that moment I shall stand
In ordain'd radiance.
A visible exaltation shall possess my limbs,
My lips shall be rosy and the porch of life,
And my eyes the light of reason.

12

Rocks
rain
riven rocks
eroded plains

Pain
anguish'd eyes
hands and lips
entreat in vain

Here is night
fabulous light
of icy stars
owlets screech

Our child is lost
in dream I have seen
a black bat lac'd
to his dead white face.

THE WHITE ISLE OF LEUCE

Leave Helen to her lover. Draw away
before the sea is dark. Frighten with your oars
the white sea-birds till they rise
on wings that veer
against the black sentinels
        of the silent wood.

The oars beat off; Achilles cannot see
the prows that dip against the dim shore's line.
But the rowers as they rest on the lifting waves
hear the revelry of Helen and a voice singing
of battle and love. The rowers hear and rest
and tremble for the limbs of Helen and the secrets of the
        sacred isle.

TOURISTS IN A SACRED PLACE

A pallid rout stepping like phantoms
beneath the arching boughs
have come with angel hands and wretched voices
to the valley and this choir of perish'd stones.

Valid was my anguish—as though a turbulent dove
had scatter'd the leafy silence.
Now in airless vistas, dim and blind my limbs will loiter
while the senses stray to vast defeats.

A rocking bell
peals in a grey tower.
The sound has broken down the strong defences
of age and innocence.

Cecily come with your virginal tremors
Cecily still the bell.
Your tresses are wet from the rushing river
a green weed clings like a vein on your breast.

Cecily, listen, the clangour is over
now only the burden of bees in the clover.
God and his angels have given you grace
and stamp'd your mission on your naiad face.

RITZ

(Love among the Ruins)

And suddenly the clocks rang out sang down the empty
    corridors
the lovers are aroused from their sleep.
It seemed the wind had blown the tender leaves like silver
    flecks
the tender leaves like silver flecks
against the sunlit belly of the wood.

East the ashy incense of summer
drifts across the lawn.
The couples just remember
lusty birds singing in the hedgerow at sunrise
singing till sound pierced to limbs slackly tumbled
in the abattoirs and coy fanes of love.

CRANACH

But once upon a time
the oakleaves and the wild boars
Antonio Antonio
the old wound is bleeding.

We are in Silvertown
we have come here with a modest ambition
to know a little bit about the river
eating cheese and pickled onions on a terrace by the Thames.

Sweet Thames! the ferry glides across your bosom
like Leda's swan.
The factories ah slender graces
sly naked damsels nodding their downy plumes.

Sic et non

★

THE COMPLAINT OF HELOISE

Elle a aussi cette chose en sextant de marine.
                                    ANTONIN ARTAUD

Abelard was: God is
   my love, I his
learned lass. But God is
   not near.

Abelard my lover
   was. I felt the
lusts that burnt us were
   too sweet:

I feared they could not last.
   I saw them pass
shedding brands to harass
   my life.

They went: cruelly forc'd.
   That he should know
doom of flesh, unique loss!
   Dear me!

I could show a white face,
   a pious dress;
but very flowers in my breast
   all fresh.

- Pluck them. God pluck them. I
   plucked them madly.
But ever burgeon'd rose,
   lily:

All the emblems
   of my distress.
God help me to hide them
   now.

THE PORTRAIT OF ABELARD

The wild boars are grubbing for acorns
Among the moist fallen leaves,
And the Arduzon disperses
Mist along its course.
The Paraclete is cold;
   the cloisters comfortless.

The eunuch is contrite;
His genitals are gone to dust—
Like amputated limbs are burnt
These twenty years in acid earth.
The river runs
   along the horizontal light.

His mind is foster'd on the infinite;
His voice is gentle, animate
With intellectual faith.
The flowers toss
   against his moving feet.

The body when depriv'd of lust
Offers to an outer God
Its forced immaculation.
The scaly sky
   hath cast its glittering sheath

And now the illumination of the stars
Visits with raw radiance
The body's hollow cave.

There bounds the fleshy sphere
More playfully
   sapp'd of seminal rheum.

PENUMBRA

In this teashop
they seem so violent.
Why should they come here
dressed for tragedy?

Did they anticipate
this genteel atmosphere?
Her eyes are like moth-wings
furtive under a black arch.

She drinks a cup of tea.
But he is embarrassed—
stretches his gross neck
out of the white grip of his collar.

Sits uneasily
eagerly rises now she has done.
Anxiously seeks the looking-glass
then seeks the door.

She is gone
a vestal her robes fluttering
like a printed sheet
in a gusty Tube.

THE JUDGEMENT OF MICHAEL

He is Saint Michael of the flaming sword
His curl'd head wreath'd in flame.

His wings with a myriad curving blades
Cut and climb the cloudy air.

His sword is terrible and high:
The devil is a distraught worm.

O yellow flame of swift blade!
O red and inwrith'd worm!

LEPIDOPTERA

These pink chrysalid faces
devoid of anything so atavistic as whiskers
flame evenly beneath felt hats—
abash'd torches in the daylight.

Intent on solemn inanities
they maintain a torpid demeanour

Until night finally falls
when stript of their drab or tinsel sheaths
they ape Narcissus in mildewed mirrors
display their graces to the sick glare of gas-jets
and on rococo quilts
get corybantic for a while.

EARLY ASTIR

Early, early I walked in the city:
The river ran its strength from misty valleys
and the sun lit the wings of stone angels.

Yarrol! Yarrol! I cried exultingly:
Passing dogs lifted wet noses
and housemaidens the blinds of their gables.

PICARESQUE

Limbs
   legs of caravaners
      steam-boaters picnickers

Winged arms
   of walkers
Are tented above the impious pools
of memory.

He cannot disentangle
the genesis of any scope

HIS limbs
dangle
like marionettes'
over
   a
     mauve
sea.

HUSKISSON IN ARCADIA

Early dawn and the nymphs are gliding
in an elusive sequence
of gold light along the woodland's edge;
and the songs
of rousèd birds are making
dawn vocal in leafy domes.

Huskisson is yet sleeping.
When at last light slits his puffy lids
the nymphs have taken to their far recesses
and birds are busy on their wings.

But soon he takes his whittled stick
and goes into the early morning.
Down the lane to the garth-pen
he urges the mournful milky cattle.

The milkmaids meet them in the sheds
with bright-scoured pails and milking stools.
They lean their pretty heads
against a cow's roan glossy flank
and languidly impel
the juicy dugs.

Huskisson leaves for the meadows
where the woolly ewes munch cool grass.
Koy-bé, koy-bé, he calls to the lambs
who bleat in the wild loneliness.

he lifts the old ewes' feet to scrape the rot
and scatters fresh swedes for them to eat.

The peewits cry, the sun climbs high
Huskisson is gay in the meadows.

A MAIDEN'S COMEDY

Don Roderigo took her fancy
As he flaunted his cloak on the highway:
She gave him a curtsey, not knowing why,
And he answered her with a 'Good-day'.

Don Roderigo halted then his wandering
And sang in the petalled orchard his intent:
'If the night's pellucid we will walk
Till the stars relent.'

Don Roderigo hid the stars
With his cloak like ravens' wings:
He walked with a maid's virginity
And regaled her with all manner of things.

DEVICE

O that I might believe that time
Is but a measure thrown on things
That hold existence in a sphere
Intense alone, and always felt
In full reality! For then
I could evade despondency
By magnifying to my frame
The ecstatic beat that night and day
Pulses within the milk-white walls
Of mental sloth, eager to break
Into the radiant release
Of vision divine and precise.

—Time that is a shrouded thought
Involving earth and life in doubt.

THE END OF A WAR
(1933)

'*In former days we used to look at life, and sometimes from a distance, at death, and still further removed from us, at eternity. Today it is from afar that we look at life, death is near us, and perhaps nearer still is eternity.*'

JEAN BOUVIER, a French subaltern
February, 1916

ARGUMENT

In the early days of November 1918, the Allied Forces had for some days been advancing in pursuit of the retreating German Army. The advance was being carried out according to a schedule. Each division was given a line to which it must attain before nightfall; and this meant that each battalion in a division had to reach a certain point by a certain time. The schedule was in general being well adhered to, but the opposition encountered varied considerably at different points.

On November 10th, a certain English Battalion had been continuously harassed by machine-gun fire, and late in the afternoon was still far from its objective. Advancing under cover, it reached the edge of a plantation from which stretched a wide open space of cultivated land, with a village in front about 500 yards away. The officer in charge of the scouts was sent ahead with a corporal and two men to reconnoitre, and this little party reached the outskirts of the village without observing any signs of occupation. At the entrance of the village, propped against a tree, they found a German officer, wounded severely in the thigh. He was quite conscious and looked up calmly as Lieut. S—— approached him. He spoke English, and when questioned, intimated that the village had been evacuated by the Germans two hours ago.

Thereupon Lieut. S—— signalled back to the battalion, who then advanced along the road in marching formation. It was nearly dusk when they reached the small place in front of the church, and there they were halted. Immediately from several points, but chiefly

99

from the tower of the church, a number of machine-guns opened fire on the massed men. A wild cry went up, and the men fled in rage and terror to the shelter of the houses, leaving a hundred of their companions and five officers dead or dying on the pavement. In the houses and the church they routed out the ambushed Germans and mercilessly bayoneted them.

The corporal who had been with Lieut. S—— ran to the entrance of the village, to settle with the wounded officer who had betrayed them. The German seemed to be expecting him; his face did not flinch as the bayonet descended.

When the wounded had been attended to, and the dead gathered together, the remaining men retired to the schoolhouse to rest for the night. The officers then went to the château of the village, and there in a gardener's cottage, searching for fuel, the corporal already mentioned found the naked body of a young girl. Both legs were severed, and one severed arm was found in another room. The body itself was covered with bayonet wounds. When the discovery was reported to Lieut. S——, he went to verify the strange crime, but there was nothing to be done; he was, moreover, sick and tired. He found a bed in another cottage near the château, where some old peasants were still cowering behind a screen. He fell into a deep sleep, and did not wake until the next morning, the 11th of November, 1918.

MEDITATION OF A DYING
GERMAN OFFICER

Ich sterbe. . . . Life ebbs with an easy flow
and I've no anguish now. This failing light
is the world's light: it dies like a lamp
flickering for want of oil. When the last jump comes
and the axe-head blackness slips through flesh
that welcomes it with open but unquivering lips
then I shall be one with the Unknown
this Nothing which Heinrich made his argument
for God's existence: a concept beyond the mind's reach.
But why embody the Unknown: why give to God
anything but essence, intangible, invisible, inert?
The world is full of solid creatures—these
are the mind's material, these we must mould
into images, idols to worship and obey:
The Father and the Flag, and the wide Empire
of our creative hands. I have seen
the heart of Europe send its beating blood
like a blush over the world's pallid sphere
calling it to one life, one order and one living.
For that dream I've given my life and to the last
fought its listless enemies. Now Chaos intervenes
and I leave not gladly but with harsh disdain
a world too strong in folly for the bliss of dreams.

I fought with gladness. When others cursed the day
this stress was loosed
and men were driven into camps, to follow
with wonder, woe, or base delirium
the voiceless yet incessant surge
then I exulted: but with not more
than a nostril's distension, an eager eye
and fast untiring step.

                                    The first week
I crossed the Fatherland, to take my place

in the swift-wing'd swoop that all but ended
the assay in one wild and agile venture.
I was blooded then, but the wound
seared in the burning circlet of my spirit
served only to temper courage
with scorn of action's outcome.
Blooded but not beaten I left the ranks
to be a leader. Four years
I have lived in the ecstasy of battle.
The throbbing of guns, growing yearly,
has been drum music to my ears
the crash of shells the thrill of cymbals
bayonets fiddlers' bows and the crack of rifles
plucked harp strings. Now the silence
is unholy. Death has no deeper horror
than diminishing sound—ears that strain
for the melody of action, hear
only the empty silence of retreating life.
Darkness will be kinder.

                                             I die—
But still I hear a distant gunfire, stirring in my ear
like a weary humming nerve. I will cling to that sound
and on its widening wave
lapse into eternity. Heinrich, are you near?
Best friend, but false to my faith
would you die doubtfully with so calm a gaze?
Mind above battles, does your heart resign
love of the Fatherland in this hour of woe?
No drum will beat in your dying ears, and your God
will meet you with a cold embrace.
The void is icy: your Abstraction
freezes the blood at death: no calm
bound in such a barren law. The bond between
two human hearts is richer. Love can seal
the anguish'd ventricles with subtle fire
and make life end in peace, in love
the love we shared in all this strife.
Heinrich, your God has not this power, or he would heal

the world's wounds and create the empire
now left in the defeated hands of men.

At Valenciennes I saw you turn
swiftly into an open church. I followed
stood in the shadow of the aisle
and watched you pray. My impulse then
was to meet you in the porch and test
my smile against your smile, my peace against yours
and from your abashment pluck a wilder hope.
But the impulse died in the act: your face was blank
drained of sorrow as of joy, and I was dumb
before renunciation's subtler calm.
I let you pass, and into the world
went to deny my sight, to seal my lips
against the witness of your humble faith.
For my faith was action: is action now!
In death I triumph with a deed
and prove my faith against your passive ghost.

Faith in self comes first, from self we build
the web of friendship, from friends to confederates
and so to the State. This web has a weft
in the land we live in, a town, a hill
all that the living eyes traverse. There are lights
given by the tongue we speak, the songs we sing,
the music and the magic of our Fatherland.
This is a tangible trust. To make it secure
against the tempests of inferior minds
to build it in our blood, to make our lives
a tribute to its beauty—there is no higher aim.
This good achieved, then to God we turn
for a crown on our perfection: God we create
in the end of action, not in dreams.

God dies in this dying light. The mists receive
my spent spirit: there is no one to hear

my last wish. Already my thoughts
rebound in a tenement whose doors
are shut: strange muscles clench my jaws
these limbs are numb. I cannot lift
a finger to my will. But the mind
rises like a crystal sphere above the rigid wreck
is poised there, perhaps to fall into the void
still dreaming of an Empire of the West.
And so still feels no fear! Mind triumphs over flesh
ordering the body's action in direst danger.
Courage is not born in men, but born of love
love of life and love of giving, love
of this hour of death, which all love seeks.

I die, but death was destined. My life was given
my death ordained when first my hand
held naked weapons in this war. The rest
has been a waiting for this final hour.
In such a glory I could not always live.

My brow falls like a shutter of lead, clashes
on the clench'd jaw. The curtain of flesh
is wreathed about these rigid lines
in folds that have the easy notion of a smile.
So let them kiss earth and acid corruption:
extinction of the clod. The bubble is free
to expand to the world's confines or to break
against the pricking stars. The last lights shine
across its perfect crystal: rare ethereal glimmer
of mind's own intensity. Above the clod
all things are clear, and what is left
is petulant scorn, implanted passions,
everything not tensely ideal. Blind emotions
wreck the image with their blundering wings.
Mind must define before the heart intrigues.

Last light above the world, wavering in the darkest
void of Nothing—how still and tenuous

no music of the spheres—and so break with a sigh
against the ultimate
shores of this world
so finite
so small
Nichts

DIALOGUE BETWEEN THE BODY AND
THE SOUL OF THE MURDERED GIRL

BODY

I speak not from my pallid lips
but from these wounds.

SOUL

Red lips that cannot tell
a credible tale.

BODY

In a world of martyr'd men
these lips renounce their ravage:
The wounds of France
roused their fresh and fluid voices.

SOUL

War has victims beyond the bands
bonded to slaughter. War moves with armoured wheels
across the quivering flesh and patient limbs
of all life's labile fronds.

BODY

France was the garden I lived in.
Amid these trees, these fields, petals fell
flesh to flesh; I was a wilder flower.

SOUL

Open and innocent. So is the heart
laid virgin to my choice. I filled

your vacant ventricles with dreams
with immortal hopes and aspirations that exalt
the flesh to passion, to love and hate.
Child-radiance then is clouded, the light
that floods the mind is hot with blood
pulse beats to the vibrant battle-cry
the limbs are burnt with action.

BODY

The heart had not lost its innocence so soon
but for the coming of that day when men
speaking a strange tongue, wearing strange clothes
armed, flashing with harness and spurs
carrying rifles, lances or spears
followed by rumbling waggons, shrouded guns
passed through the village in endless procession
swift, grim, scornful, exulting.

SOUL

You had not lost your innocence so soon
but for the going of men from the village
your father gone, your brother
only the old left, and the very young
the women sad, the houses shuttered
suspense of school, even of play
the eager search for news, the air
of universal doubt, and then the knowledge
that the wavering line of battle now was fixed
beyond this home. The soil was tilled
for visionary hate.

BODY

Four years was time enough
for such a seedling hate to grow
sullen, close, intent;
To wait and wonder
but to abate
no fervour in the slow passage of despair.

106

The mind grew tense.

My wild flesh was caught
in the cog and gear of hate.

I lay coiled, the spring
of all your intricate design.

You served me well. But still I swear
Christ was my only King.

France was your Motherland:
To her you gave your life and limbs.

I gave these hands and gave these arms
I gave my head of ravelled hair.

You gave your sweet round breasts
like Agatha who was your Saint.

Mary Aegyptiaca
is the pattern of my greatest loss.

To whom in nakedness and want
God sent a holy man.
Who clothed her, shrived her, gave her peace
before her spirit left the earth.

BODY

My sacrifice was made to gain
the secrets of these hostile men.

SOUL

I hover round your fameless features
barred from Heaven by light electric.

BODY

All men who find these mauled remains
will pray to Mary for your swift release.

SOUL

The cry that left your dying lips
was heard by God.

BODY

I died for France.

SOUL

A bright mantle fell across your bleeding limbs.
Your face averted shone with sacred fire.
So be content. In this war
many men have perished not bless'd
with faith in a cause, a country or a God
not less martyrs than Herod's Victims, Ursula's Virgins
or any mass'd innocents massacred.

BODY

Such men give themselves not to their God but to their fate
die thinking the face of God not love but hate.

SOUL

Those who die for a cause die comforted and coy;
believing their cause God's cause they die with joy.

MEDITATION OF THE WAKING
ENGLISH OFFICER

I wake: I am alive: there is a bell
sounding with the dream's retreating surf
O catch the lacey hem dissolv'd in light
that creeps along the healing tendrils of a mind
still drugg'd with sleep. Why must my day
kill my dreams? Days of hate. But yes a bell
beats really on this air, a mad bell.
The peasants stir behind that screen.
Listen: they mutter now: they sing
in their old crackt voices, intone
a litany. There are no guns
only these voices of thanksgiving. Can it be?
Yes yes yes: it is peace, peace!
The world is very still, and I am alive!
Alive, alive, alive. . . .
O limbs, your white radiance
no longer to stand against bloody shot
this heart secure, to live and worship
to go God's way, to grow in faith
to fight with and not against the will!
That day has come at last! Suspended life
renews its rhythmic beat. I live!
Now can I love and strive, as I have dreamt.

Lie still, and let this litany
of simple voices and the jubilant bell
ease rebirth. First there are the dead to bury
O God, the dead. How can God's bell
ring out from that unholy ambush?
That tower of death! In excess of horror
war died. The nerve was broken
fray'd men fought obscenely then: there was no fair joy
no glory in the strife, no blessed wrath.
Man's mind cannot excel

mechanic might except in savage sin.
Our broken bodies oiled the engines: mind was grit.

Shall I regret my pact? Envy that friend
who risked ignominy, insult, gaol
rather than stain his hands with human blood?
And left his fellow men. Such lonely pride
was never mine. I answered no call
there was no call to answer. I felt no hate
only the anguish of an unknown fate
a shot, a cry: then armies on the move
the sudden lull in daily life
all eyes wide with wonder, past surprise:
our felt dependence on a ruling few:
the world madness: the wild plunge:
the avalanche and I myself a twig
torn from its mother soil
and to the chaos rendered.
                                        Listless
I felt the storm about me; its force
too strong to beat against; in its swirl
I spread my sapling arms, toss'd on its swell
I rose, I ran, I down the dark world sped
till death fell round me like a rain of steel
and hope and faith and love coiled in my inmost cell.

Often in the weariness of watching
warding weary men, pitch'd against
the unmeaning blackness of the night, the wet fog,
the enemy blanketed in mystery, often
I have questioned my life's inconstant drift;
God not real, hate not real, the hearts of men
insentient engines pumping blood
into a spongy mass that cannot move
above the indignity of inflicted death:
the only answer this: the infinite is all
and I, a finite speck, no essence even
of the life that falls like dew

from the spirit breathed on the fine edge
of matter, perhaps only that edge
a ridge between eternal death and life eternal
a moment of time, temporal.
The universe swaying between Nothing and Being
and life faltering like a clock's tick
between a pendulum's coming and going.
The individual lost: seventy years
seventy minutes, have no meaning.
Let death, I cried, come from the forward guns
let death come this moment, swift and crackling
tick-tock, tick-tock—moments that pass
not reckoned in the infinite.

Then I have said: all is that must be.
There is no volition, even prayer
dies on lips compress'd in fear.
Where all must be, there is no God
for God can only be the God of prayer
an infinitely kind Father whose will
can mould the world, who can
in answer to my prayer, mould me.
But whilst I cannot pray, I can't believe
but in this frame of machine necessity
must renounce not only God, but self.
For what is the self without God?
A moment not reckoned in the infinite.
My soul is less than nothing, lost,
unless in this life it can build
a bridge to life eternal.

In a warm room, by the flickering fire
in friendly debate, in some remote
shelter'd existence, even in the hermit's cell
easy it is to believe in God: extend the self
to communion with the infinite, the eternal.
But haggard in the face of death
deprived of all earthly comfort, all hope of life,

the soul a distill'd essence, held
in a shaking cup, spilt
by a spit of lead, saved
by chance alone
very real
in its silky bag of skin, its bond of bone,
so little and so limited,
there's no extenuation then.
Fate is in facts: the only hope
an unknown chance.

So I have won through. What now?
Will faith rise triumphant from the wreck
despair once more evaded in a bold
assertion of the self: self to God related
self in God attain'd, self a segment
of the eternal circle, the wheel
of Heaven, which through the dust of days
and stagnant darkness steadily revolves?

Your gentian eyes stared from the cold
impassive alp of death. You betrayed us
at the last hour of the last day
a smile your only comment
on the well-done deed. What mind
have you carried over the confines?
Your fair face was noble of its kind
some visionary purpose cut the lines
clearly on that countenance.
But you are defeated: once again
the meek inherit the kingdom of God.
No might can win against this wandering
wavering grace of humble men.
You die, in all your power and pride:
I live, in my meekness justified.

When first this fury caught us, then
I vowed devotion to the rights of men

would fight for peace once it came again
from this unwilled war pass gallantly
to wars of will and justice.
That was before I had faced death
day in day out, before hope had sunk
to a little pool of bitterness.
Now I see, either the world is mechanic force
and this the last tragic act, portending
endless hate and blind reversion
back to the tents and healthy lusts
of animal men: or we act
God's purpose in an obscure way.
Evil can only to the Reason stand
in scheme or scope beyond the human mind.
God seeks the perfect man, plann'd
to love him as a friend: our savage fate
a fire to burn our dross
to temper us to finer stock
man emerging in some inconceived span
as something more than remnant of a dream.

To that end worship God, join the voices
heard by these waking ears. God is love:
in his will the meek heart rejoices
doubting till the final grace a dove
from Heaven descends and wakes the mind
in light above the light of human kind
in light celestial
infinite and still
eternal
bright

POEMS 1914–1934
(1935)

INBETWEENTIMES

Between the Winter and the Spring
between day and night
a no man's time a mean light
with cold mist creeping along the alleys
and the sun like a world withdrawn.

The shrill voices of surplus children
shake up the frosty dust
lamps are lit
and bleak shadows like bruises
rise under their golden eyes.

Through these cavernous streets
between a winter and a spring
between night and day
we wander our hearts lifted
above the shadows and the dust
secure in an alien light.

SEPTEMBER FIRES

Haulms burn
in distant fields.
Reluctantly the plumes of smoke
rise against a haze
of hills blue and clear
but featureless.

Our feet
crush the crinkled beech-leaves.
There is no other life than ours.
God is good to us this September evening
to give us a sun
and a world burning its dross.

Let us burn the twisted years
that have brought us to this meeting.
The crops are cull'd—
we can expect no other fruit
until another year
brings fire and fealty and the earth in barren stillness.

THE EVEN SKEIN

Ragged ends
are the world's ends: land in water, wind-woven branches,
sea-spray, star-fret, any atmosphere;
and everywhere
where mind meets matter, fray'd nerves
and tender fingers, feeling the stone's jagged edge;
ragged ends of love
that can never be complete,
secret meetings, interrupted speech,
broken handshakes
and the shuffle of reluctant feet
down alleys where the broken light
falls brokenly
on broken walls.

Ragged ends of life that has no aim
but plucks its flowers with a ragged stem
perhaps arranges them
in a bowl of clouded glass
where for a day or two
they stand exulting on console, sill or mantelpiece
then fade
into a dry and brittle ghost.

Ragged ends of time
that no time will knit together.
Death is the only even skein:
Death that is both ghost and gain.

DAY'S AFFIRMATION

Emerging at midnight
to cool my aching eyes with the sight of stars
I hear the nightingale
throbbing in the thicket by my garden gate

and I think:
A poet in the old days would have made a song
of your song and the starlit night
the scent of wallflowers clinging to the ground.

But now it is different:
you sing but we are silent
our hearts too sadly patient
all these years.

Sing on! The night is cool.
Morning and the world will be lit
with whitebeam candles shining and O the frail
and tender daring splendour of wild cherrytrees.

NIGHT'S NEGATION

Trees
have held these flecks of light
    these brittle stars that in the night
flash
    on the unfolding fans of space

Blue fans
that bring me peace
    and nerves that cease
to feel
    the torture of day's lease

of life and lust. O day that hurt
   the heart and pillag'd the short
      and shatter'd frame of good report

O noon that bled
   till night had led
      the lover's limbs to love's deathbed.

THE SEVEN SLEEPERS

The seven sleepers ere they left
the light and colour of the earth
the seven sleepers they did cry
(banishing their final fears):

'Beauty will not ever fade.
To our cavern we retire
doom'd to sleep ten thousand years.
Roll the rock across the gap

Then forget us; we are quiet:
stiff and cold our bodies lie;
Earth itself shall stir ere we
visit Earth's mortality.

Beauty when we wake will be
a solitude on land and sea.'

TIME REGAINED

The limbs remember blood and fire:
a hurt that's done may in the mind
sink and lose identity;

for the mind has reasons of its own
for covering with an eyeless mask
marks of mortality.

The limbs remember fire and joy
and flesh to flesh is benison
of entity;

but the mind has reasons of its own
for circumventing life and love's
sodality.

LEGEND

(for Viola and Pianoforte: Bax)

This X
bland above her breast
is no holy cross
but the crest of sacrifice

Some sacred instinct
unfolds the frond
of sullen sound
Now the air

is anguish
Beauty is born
a wailing child
held high

above the crystal
bastion high
above the geometry of tendons
round which the blue veins twine

The eyes are shut
the brow
taut
in the equation of joy and pain

Through expectant space
falls a tender flail
tense the bow
sings after its expended

fiery arrows
The laws of steel
are static now
the labile life of blood returns

the ulterior crane
swings into rest
its load of sifted sound
the body turns

OTHER

Other faces
   are like lamps unlit:
yours is a net
   in which a thousand stars are caught;
the sky around
   is darker for their deft withdrawal.

Other voices
    are a dead monotony:
yours is the rapt cry
    of the Sistine singers building an echo
high in vaults
    where the Sibyl reads from an open scroll.

Other lives
    drift to the Sirens' rock:
your music
    issues in the wind's wake
muted and immortal
    as the murmur from the Triton's coil'd shell.

AUBADE

Early light
beats down

my body is a beaten
silver leaf

If I rise
it will wrinkle
a tinsel pod

a wither'd caul
from the womb of night

NIGHT RIDE

Along the black
leather strap
of the night
deserted road

swiftly rolls
the freighted bus.
Huddled together
two lovers doze

their hands linkt
across their laps
their bodies loosely
interlockt

their heads resting
two heavy fruits
on the plaited
basket of their limbs.

Slowly the bus
slides into light.
Here are hills
detach'd from dark

the road uncoils
a white ribbon
the lovers with
the hills unfold

wake cold
to face the fate
of those who love
despite the world.

FLIGHT

The serial feathers
imbricated
conceal the struts

an extending
N: flex'd;
when taut

folding air
coiling the currents
never bending

till the body
seeks the level
of its rest.

TENEMENT

Third block
four up
the window shut
blank uncurtain'd

other windows
glint grin
all sinister
within

reflect
rainy clouds
uncertain tracery
of winter twigs

a wire sings
an insulator
clings
like a wren to the wall

MELVILLE

Melville fell
and the albatross
out of the rigging

Edam the moon
all angular else
mast and ropes

a feather fell
a claw
clutched the ladder

slipped
Melville fell
forty fathoms Melville fell

fathoms below the sea level

GIOVANNI DI PAOLO

Levels ledges
a filter of ditches
falling the terraces

edg'd with rock
then the plain
pattern'd with pennants

diagonals of walls
waterways vine-poles
the ghastly Golgotha

against it all

TECTIFORM

In this extensive gloom
foxes nest
under concrete ashlars

fallen like broken blades
half-in half-out
the tangled rusty steel

A raven rides
the rooftree settling down
angle of 63

ends flex'd gaunt
like accents
over the dark eyes of gutted sheds

The fox runs
over the vivid quitch burying
banks of black encaustic soil

the river is flowing clear

THE INNOCENT EYE

Potential
mirror of gentle acts
agents of factual
joy

enjoy
deft engines
but shade yourself
against electric signs

that in the night
destroy the stars
and lurid phantoms
feature on hotel stairs.

Angelicos
diatoms
of senseful surfeit—
how can man deny you?

He should employ you
whenever
he wakes in the world
out of dusty fever

and with not worm
and weevil
for whom
God grows stavesacre

but with bird and lynx
enlarge his life
with crystal lens
and furtive lust.

HULK

After a wet season
the leaves fall early
and bells among the damsel trees
invent the dusk

We had been discussing
God and Fate and the eternal reflux:
    after the white ecstasy of intellect
    the axe, the sceptre, the tent people with bright trappings.

Your voice was the voice of the yellow sunflowers
pouring fire into the dusk;
   but above your voice the bells were rocking
   my heart beating
       with the same reiteration

flux and reflux

   Carried on this singing sea
   (my blood)
   the curv'd bones of my breast
   drift into darkness.

LOGOS

Suddenly he began to torture the flowers
began to twist red winter tulips
faced by the behemothian jaws
for which there is no inevitable IN and OUT

The carnage at the Menin Gate
the startled blackcock's raucous cry
the Morse code of a boot and crutch
filled the space between river and sky.

But stay! the light is cancelled there
the dark eyes cease
to stare at suns
and light breaks in behind the brain.

A NORTHERN LEGION

Bugle calls coiling through the rocky valley
have found echoes in the eagles' cries:
an outrage is done on anguish'd men
now men die and death is no deedful glory.

Eleven days this legion forced the ruin'd fields, the
burnt homesteads and empty garths, the broken arches
of bridges: desolation moving like a shadow before them, a
rain of ashes. Endless their anxiety

marching into a northern darkness: approaching
a narrow defile, the waters falling fearfully
the clotting menace of shadows and all the multiple
instruments of death in ambush against them.

The last of the vanguard sounds his doleful note.
The legion now is lost. None will follow.

THE NUNCIO

So our virtues
Lie in the interpretation of the time.
CORIOLANUS, iv, 7

I too was present
one of a tufted mat of men
gathered under a high coffer'd ceiling.
I stood apart, making an image
for the dense throng of heads
hard, carapaceous
inhabited by a thousand eyes
crouch'd there like a scarab body
on each side the receding
columns of porphyry and gold
outspread like tense wings.

My musings were interrupted
by a fanfare and a sudden cry of heralds.
In the ensuing silence
all eyes were drawn
to the slowly opening doors.

First to enter were two attendants
carrying a regalia of astronomical instruments.

Starr was the name of the one we waited for.
He entered presently, removing his tiara
with the economical gestures of a man entering his own
    house.

A short squat man.
his hair powder-blue
on his white shaven skull

He spoke immediately
into the ear of the microphone
he spoke immaculately
like a dancer
speaking into the ear of his partner.

'We may not have long to wait
not so very long
There has been despair: the first shock of defeat
cost us more losses in faith than in men.
Now we must build again
repair our broken parapets
dig fresh communication trenches.
The lines are cut; runners must proceed with messages.
At all costs we must make contact
assemble our scattered units
issue orders for a counter-attack.

Against tyrants there is only one weapon
anciently the pen now the microphone.

From the high tension of our minds
must radiate such measures as the situation demands.
From Moscow Princeton Berlin and Paris
from London Tokyo Rome and Buenos Ayres
from every city school and cloister
we must gather to avert disaster.

Our structures are of steel and glass
their subtle struts not obvious
we build with space in space
and by ingenuity produce
our aerial houses high towers
our winding stairs—
all is in light
above-board and ought
to win the approval of the masses.

But by those ignorant of stresses
our architecture is dismissed
as at best a jest.
Any demagogue can raise a wind
to break the logic of the mind.
In the last extremity
we can no longer employ geometry.
Floodlights of emotion
must be thrown against the recess'd terraces
the rectangular towers and bleak buttresses—
the external form of our adventure.
We must design with brighter colour
borrowing harmonies from children at school
and especially on an outer wall
cast a warmth that will appeal
to those unable to measure steel.

On our highest towers we might erect
flagpoles on which to inflict
pennants streamers and any pied
pattern that catches the colour-avid eye.

Rays of light and yards of bunting
take the place of verbal ranting.
Never to the eye deny
what the mind can amplify.

Then we must provide some stairs
obviously connect the various floors.
The lift that shoots from first to fourth
will only be a cause of wrath
to those long accustom'd to creep
from first to second step by step.

Such ascending and descending spirals
will serve eventually as treadmills
or as a substitute for war.
The lift can thread the spiral core.

We must not forget the fire-escapes
we must decoy suspicious dupes
with the prospect of continual safety
We must not treat this matter lightly:
the mouse the mole and the rabbit
have habits different from the robot.
Rodents range darkly in a fire-proof underground
not meeting fire
they have no fear.
But our enemy like an ampersand
lives inevitably *between*
between land and sky, between earth and heaven.
He must connect, and if he leaves the earth
must be assured of a safe path
back to his natural element.
A building without a fire-escape
he regards as a dangerous man-trap.

No need to multiply instances.
But we must reduce the area of glass:
we have avoided darkness
our structures are transparent—

only the skeleton visible and adamant
lies like a net embedded criss-cross
This would fail as an ambush
therefore blacken the glass
fill in the mesh
with soil and cement
any opaque element
so that their eyes cannot penetrate
partitions or discover remote
repetitions of plane and space.
Their eyes do not wish to pierce
floor or ceiling, nor traverse
limitless horizons; eyes
follow nose
fixed and unilateral in their course.

The strategy must vary
according to the class and climate
but normally provide a dormitory
where every night
your prisoners may sleep;
otherwise their weary footsteps will distract
the occupiers of the inner cells, who conduct
their meditations in despite
of earth's diurnal revolution, and the want of faith and hope.

    Thus in various ways by various devices
    sacrificing appearances preserving the reality
    evading force by the use of mental agility
    guarding in an inner redoubt under lock and key
    the lost lineaments of goodness truth and beauty.'

Starr paused, his head erect
his eyes fixed on some abstract
conception of the universe and man.
His audience was very still, and when
Starr spoke again
his whisper barely reached the microphone.

'In a vision we have seen
the world one, all men one
a single confederation
spreading from ocean to ocean

reason supreme
a flame
served by a few priests
the world obeying their behests

the evil and the ill
tamed and all
spiritual corruption
given absolution.

Reason like a lily
fed by sense and feeling
blooming eternally
ruling
all the flowers of the field

Starr ceased
and we who had listened
suspended in stillness
surged like a sudden tide
towards the dais where he stood.
But Starr
checked our rash
onward rush
held us with his lifted hand
and to us gave this last command:

'Each to his cell:
the individual
is the pivot of our plan.
God only speaks to those who pray.
Action without grace can never win.

Therefore seek grace in meditation: employ
your mind and senses in the worship
without which we are without hope.
Reason prevails
against all symbols;
symbols are idols of mind's darkest level:
live in light immune from evil.'

So Starr left us

and then in single floes and flakes
we broke apart and left that hall
each intent, each mind full
of plans, prognostications and strategics.

A SHORT POEM FOR ARMISTICE DAY

Gather or take fierce degree
trim the lamp set out for sea
here we are at the workmen's entrance
clock in and shed your eminence.

Notwithstanding, work it diverse ways
work it diverse days, multiplying four digestions
here we make artificial flowers
of paper tin and metal thread.

One eye one leg one arm one lung
a syncopated sick heart-beat
the record is not nearly worn
that weaves a background to our work.

I have no power therefore have patience
These flowers have no sweet scent
no lustre in the petal no increase
from fertilising flies and bees.

No seed they have no seed
their tendrils are of wire and grip
the buttonhole the lip
and never fade

And will not fade though life
and lustre go in genuine flowers
and men like flowers are cut
and wither on a stem

And will not fade a year or more
I stuck one in a candlestick
and there it clings about the socket
I have no power therefore have patience.

THE BROWN BOOK OF THE HITLER TERROR

In Bednib's shop I picked up a book
An actor came in in a floating gown
He gave me an objective look
I put the book down

And went into the sunlit streets
Where cars like shuttles passed my eyes
Discreet, I cried, discreet, discreet
And only Socrates was wise.

POEMS NOT PREVIOUSLY
COLLECTED 1935-40

LOVE AND DEATH

On a strange bed I drop my tired head
But sleep does not come—only wakeful dread.
The room was dark at first, but now
The light that filters from the street
Falls aslant the mirror, casts in my eyes
Its mildewed radiance. My limbs
That like a busy watch
Mark the seconds with their urgent twitch
Enlarge the area of my mind
Keep me alert to every sound
That echoes in the space
Around this unknown inn where I have come
So weary and late.

The last step outside has died away.
All is quiet, the bulbs extinct
That lately glowed above the stink and lust
Of urban life. The shadows in my room
Shift like silhouettes on frosted glass,
Coagulate and tremble into shape.
The light seems now to cut across a street
Leaving an edge of darkness round which creeps
A careless figure. She stands irresolute
Her misty breath jumping like a plume
Into the icy fog. Pellicules of dew
Which catch and concentrate the light
Have settled on the fringes of her hair;
Her step is soft and soundless as she moves
Across the cobbled street whose greasy sets
Meet her worn feet like folded knuckles.
I wait in the dark, withdrawn.
But she by instinct guided comes my way
And stands before me till her silence
Is a question, and I yield
And take her hand, and lead her to my room
Which now is suddenly light and warm.

I am not curious. I see her eyes are clear
and the tresses where the hoar has formed
Are like the withered sheaths that hang from corn.
Her dress she soon discards
And falls into my arms and laughs and cries
And tells me life was sad until I came.
She sits beside the fire; her eyes, her lips, her limbs
Speak of love, a feeling I have known
But never until this moment seen
Embodied in a form not sought but found.

Between the firelight and the lamp
Her body gleams distinct, as if it had absorbed
Ethereal rays, which now give out
Their luminous response to night.
The more she gleams and grows intense
The less I know myself—until
I am not there, except that in her mind
I dwell, and look into the world through crystal eyes
And see the swelling waves break into surf
On golden sand, and birds with bright wings
Sailing the air which shakes
The fronds and ferns on wiry stalks
Against the even green
Of endless fields.

                    A dream,
As soon I know. For then she falls asleep
Her head upon the hearth, her limbs
Like Danae's open to the fitful flame.
When I awake she is not there
And I am I again, a prickling frame
Of flesh and bone, gazing upon the earlier scene
Of drifting fog and artificial light.

But now there comes
Sidling round the selfsame edge of dark
Another figure, this time a boy

Dressed in rags, so thin
His shadow seems a blade
That cuts across the cobbled street.
He shuffles till he stands, a beggar, at my feet.
Then once again we are within the room
Now lit by sinking embers. Once again
The figure strips and stands
Lank and angular against the glow.
His eyes are sunk so deep I cannot see
Their colour, nor discover their intent.
His cheeks are drawn about his jaw
And every joint articulate.
He puts his bony hand against my breast.
I do not shrink—indeed, I feel
His still appeal and in his mind
Find a cool retreat.

The shore is icy, a cliff of glass
Against which the sullen waves
Slide in the distant lunar grip.
The seabirds cry in the white silence
And cease only when the breaking floes
Boom like a muffled gun
Across the arctic waste.
Again I find myself
My face against the worldly scene.
But now it is no dream. The fog
Drifts over the empty street.
Sleet falls across the light.
I shudder and turn. There in my bed
The lovely girl and the destitute lad
Are lying enlaced. And I know they are dead.

A DREAM

Her angel flight from cliff to lake
sustains its poise upon the sheet of silk
she holds above her head.

The air is still in dreams
a clear and plastic element.
No ripples dim the surface as she falls
the cold distress
of days unknown of days to be.

The lake receives her the lake her lover
her ravished flesh redeems the rocky floor
Still, as if asleep, she lies
a treasure to be salvaged by who dares
shatter the level mirror of the lake.

I do not dare: defeatist I have seen
the cloth she held relinquished on the lake
a baldaquin on which reposes
a neatly ravelled coil of rope.

Another runs and dives and I am free
to stay a prisoner in the timeless cell of dreams.

MAN

What is man that he moans
and makes with madness
a beaten blade

Breaks the stone with icy axe
and builds under the cliff
an imperishable tomb?

What is man that is a man
and wakes out of a dream
in the leaden dawn

But a wanderer with a silver tongue
distilling illusion and weak delight
under a yellow sun?

Beyond is a margin of planetary rings
a bowl of blue space
and then?

A vision that slowly grows dim
and eyelids that close at an end
of wonder and pain.

THE DEATH OF A STATESMAN

Despise him? No! We have not read
The meter of his pain; nor know
The path drilled through a fevered brain
By anguish, shame and sorrow.

He was not young: we must remember
Sixty years had left their score
In dark rings that dead emotions
Seared round his inmost core.

If pressed too far our nerves will slacken
And leave the will without a frame;
Mind clutches at some ignoble notion
And fears to give the fact a name.

A soul sinks to the level of its load
Which we who watch refuse to weigh;
If pressed too far we too might hear
Death sirens calling, and obey.

THIRTY-FIVE POEMS
(1940)

BOMBING CASUALTIES IN SPAIN

Dolls' faces are rosier but these were children
their eyes not glass but gleaming gristle
dark lenses in whose quicksilvery glances
the sunlight quivered. These blench'd lips
were warm once and bright with blood
but blood
held in a moist bleb of flesh
not spilt and spatter'd in tousled hair.

In these shadowy tresses
red petals did not always
thus clot and blacken to a scar.
These are dead faces.
Wasps' nests are not so wanly waxen
wood embers not so greyly ashen.

They are laid out in ranks
like paper lanterns that have fallen
after a night of riot
extinct in the dry morning air.

A SONG FOR THE SPANISH ANARCHISTS

The golden lemon is not made
    but grows on a green tree:
A strong man and his crystal eyes
    is a man born free.

The oxen pass under the yoke
    and the blind are led at will:
But a man born free has a path of his own
    and a house on the hill.

And men are men who till the land
    and women are women who weave:
Fifty men own the lemon grove
    and no man is a slave.

HERSCHEL GRYNSZPAN

This beautiful assassin is your friend:
his action the delivery of love
with magnitude in the unblemish'd years
when hate and scorn and lust
are buried under the leaves of dread.

He lifts his hand in calm despair.
The gesture loses its solitary grace
and violence is answered by violence
until the sluggish tinder of the world's indifference
is consumed, consumed to the end.

Anger is now action. The white flame of justice
will dance wildly over Europe's dark marshes
until the morning air is everywhere
and clear
as on the hills of Hellas.

This beautiful assassin is your friend
walking and whispering in the night beside you.
His voice is the voice that made you
listen to secrets in the night around you.
The light of worlds beyond your world
beguiled you with hope of a harmony
wider than the anguish of our broken lives.
The wreckage of the day was hidden.

This beautiful assassin is my friend
because my heart is filled with the same fire.

We have sheltered under the same portico
listening to the silver voice of wisdom.

Our feet faltered among the fallen stones
where once the Vandals passed
and we found
under a vivid screen of leaves
the blood still warm from a martyr's wound.

.

SUMMER RAIN

Against the window pane
against the temple of my brain
beat the muffled taps of rain.

Upon the scorch'd and mottled leaves
upon the blench'd and pented sheaves
the land receives

the liquid flood:
water like a blush of blood
returns to the parch'd rood.

The fox has left his fetid hovel
to lick the drench'd blades of sorrel;
odours rise from thyme and fennel.

The worm in his retreat deep under
the earth's insipid crust
hearing a distant drumming thunder

blindly renews his upward undulation.
The soil respires as if in emulation
of living things. All elements their maculation

desire and achieve. A warm breath
issues from the nostrils beneath
the mask of death.

TO A CONSCRIPT OF 1940

Qui n'a pas une fois désespéré de l'honneur, ne sera
jamais un héros.
GEORGE BERNANOS

A soldier passed me in the freshly fallen snow
His footsteps muffled, his face unearthly gray;
And my heart gave a sudden leap
As I gazed on a ghost of five-and-twenty years ago.

I shouted Halt! and my voice had the old accustom'd ring
And he obeyed it as it was obeyed
In the shrouded days when I too was one
Of an army of young men marching

Into the unknown. He turned towards me and I said:
'I am one of those who went before you
Five-and-twenty years ago: one of the many who never re-
    turned,
Of the many who returned and yet were dead.

We went where you are going, into the rain and the mud;
We fought as you will fight
With death and darkness and despair;
We gave what you will give—our brains and our blood.

We think we gave in vain. The world was not renewed.
There was hope in the homestead and anger in the streets
But the old world was restored and we returned
To the dreary field and workshop, and the immemorial feud

Of rich and poor. Our victory was our defeat.
Power was retained where power had been misused
And youth was left to sweep away
The ashes that the fires had strewn beneath our feet.

But one thing we learned: there is no glory in the deed
Until the soldier wears a badge of tarnish'd braid;
There are heroes who have heard the rally and have seen
The glitter of a garland round their head.

Theirs is the hollow victory. They are deceived.
But you, my brother and my ghost, if you can go
Knowing that there is no reward, no certain use
In all your sacrifice, then honour is reprieved.

To fight without hope is to fight with grace,
The self reconstructed, the false heart repaired.'
Then I turned with a smile, and he answered my salute
As he stood against the fretted hedge, which was like white
    lace.

EPITAPH

Yes yes
and ever it will come to this:
Life folds like a fan with a click!
The hand that lately beat the air
with an arch of painted silk
falls listless in the lap.

The air
the agitation and the flush
close and collapse. A rigid frame
restricts the limbs that once ran free
across the heath across the fields
over the threatening hills.

A WORLD WITHIN A WAR
(1944)

ODE

Written during the battle of Dunkirk, May, 1940

I

Fair now this world of peace
this May sun rising over the quicken'd birds
giving the tender leaves
a human warmth: opening
with golden fingers the heart of the rose.

Gently, ceaselessly, the fretted oaks
sway against the sky: not a bough or leaf
is still. The slender grasses
shiver in urgent freshness.

A butterfly desperately clings
to the shaking bell of a hyacinth.
On the sunned earth
an Iceland poppy has shed its petals
they shrivel in the heat
soon to disintegrate
cell by cell
in the slow material
kiss of death.

The same sun once sucked the film
out of the fallen seed: the mastic phlegm
flooded the dry fibre: there was life
and growth, colour and form. There was man
a coral plasm clinging to shafts of bone
fragile flesh that will fall
like a petal on the provident soil.

The mystery could end there
in birth and death, in wax and wane
and in all that for the interim
dazzles the world with bloom.

157

But just as the cool luminous clouds
inexplicably thicken in the clear air
to drift across the sun like ragged clots
spreading darkness over the green and eminent land
so there rises in the flesh of man
a forest lust: the rosy fanes
are flush'd with a darker blood: the human bond
is broken, the race divided. The petals
no longer lie withering where they fall
but are torn and crush'd, and into the soil
mashed rawly.

2

The old guns
barked into my ear. Day and night
they shook the earth in which I cowered
or rained round me
detonations of steel and fire.

One of the dazed and disinherited
I crawled out of that mess
with two medals and a gift of blood-money.
No visible wounds to lick—only a resolve
to tell the truth without rhetoric
the truth about war and about men
involved in the indignities of war.

But the world was tired and would forget
forget the pain and squalor
forget the hunger and dread
forget the cry of those who died in agony
and the unbearable silence of those who suddenly
as we talked
fell sniped
with mouth still open and uncomprehending eyes.

It is right to forget
sights the mind cannot accommodate

terror that cannot be described
experience that cannot be exorcised in thought.

It is natural for others to resent
the parade of wounds
eyes haunted with unrevealed sorrows
the unholy pride of sacrifice.

Human to relapse
into the old ways, to resume
the normality so patiently acquired
in days of peace.

And so we drifted twenty years
down the stream of time
feeling that such a storm
could not break again.

Feeling that our little house-boat was safe
until the last lock was reached.
Another twenty years
would see us home.

The day passes
the sun swerves
silently like a cyclist round the bend.
Disembodied voices drift past behind the hedge
the vespers of the blackbird and the thrush
rise and die. A golden frog
leaps out of the grasses.

In the silence of the twilight
I hear in the distance
the new guns.
I listen, no longer apt in war
unable to distinguish between bombs and shells.

As the evening deepens
searchlights begin to waver in the sky
the airplanes throb invisibly above me.
There is still a glow in the west
and Venus shines brightly over the wooded hill.

Unreal war! No single friend
links me with its immediacy.
It is a voice out of a cabinet
a printed sheet, and these faint reverberations
selected in the silence
by my attentive ear.

Presently I shall sleep
and sink into deeper oblivion.

3

Belief without action
action without thought
the blind intervention
of years without design.

We have known that a certain way of life was good
the easy salutation, the open hand
the sober disquisition, the frank eye
the unfailing satisfaction
of water wine and bread.

A step as measur'd
as a sower's on the field
quiet voices, voices of children
benedictions of women, ministrations
of gentle fingers
a centre to the circle
of all our wanderings.
And from this centre
the mind leaving the placid body
freely to range in thought and fantasy.

The world our person
the self the nucleus
the inner kernel round which
the films and shells are wrapt
deceptive or protective.

Our person our world
flex'd limbs, elastic muscles
flow and flood, ripple of breath and blood
against the skeleton's brittle wall
eye's eagerness, lickerous tongue
ear's selection, finger's fine division
all senses single and combin'd
construing the living scene
extending and contracting
finding
the livid elements the languorous the sublime.

These elements accepted but not guarded
faith formulated but not maintain'd
twenty years
without design.

4

This is the hour of retribution
the city shaken, the power taken
from palsied hands.

This is the hour of retribution
the last farewell and the repetition
of the father's sacrifice.

This is the hour of retribution
of power without pity, of work without reward
of poetry without rhetoric.

This is the hour of retribution
the sense of glory kindled, dwindling in the steel cabin
chok'd with burnt petrol.

L   161

This is the hour of retribution
the leap from earth, ecstasy in the air
the quickly withering nerve.

This is the hour of retribution
for young men in uniform, for old men in slacks
for children at play.

This is the hour of retribution
the hour of doom, the hour of extreme unction
the hour of death.

5

Happy are those who can relieve
suffering with prayer
Happy those who can rely on God
to see them through.

They can wait patiently for the end.

But we who have put our faith
in the goodness of man
and now see man's image debas'd
lower than the wolf or the hog—

Where can we turn for consolation?

6

The forts have all been taken and the last river cross'd
our cities have fallen our defenders are dead
now we must have faith in the children of the nations
and in Time which for the tyrant is a talisman of dread.

He has put down a people but the people will rise again
like water living water rising through the sand.
He has destroy'd their poets their seers and imagemakers
but others will be born and their works will withstand

the advance of armies that have power but no grace
the peril of persecution and sudden secret death
dispersion and destruction fire and brute burial.
For against his symbol is the spirit and the spirit is a breath

that rises invincible to seek reincarnation
in flesh that cannot be defeated in hearts that rescind
the powers without persuasion the hands without art
to reign in aeons that are ageless in worlds without end.

7

Persevere through despair.
If in danger
faith is maintain'd
the instruments of attainment
form in a furnace
fiercer than war.

The self, passively receiving
illusion and despair
excluding
the unreal power of symbols
the false shelter of institutions
returns reluctantly upon its self
grows like a bud
petal by petal
exfoliated from an infinite centre
the outer layers bursting and withering
the inner pressure increasing
seeking the light
and the flush of colour born of light.

The root deep in the dark soil of the past
but deeper in the unform'd future
is folded the flower.

The sun
has a hot dry breath.

8

Shield the shoot
interpose a misty veil
water the root
this flower shall exhale
its scented peace
bringing to the war-weary world
the perennial release
from fear.

The self perfected
tranquil as a dove
the heart elected
to mutual aid.

Reason and love
incurv'd like a prow
a blade dividing
time's contrary flow.

Poetry a pennon
rippling above
in the fabulous wind.

WAR AND PEACE

The kind of war is chang'd: the crusade heart
out-shatter'd: flesh a stain on broken earth
and death an unresisted rain.

The horror loos'd all honour is lost.
Peace has pride and passion: but no evil
to equal the indignity of war, whose ringing anvil
wins only anguish. The weighted hammer
breaks the stretch'd tendons at the wrist

And leaves the soul a twisted nail
tearing the flesh that still would live
and give to words the brutal edge of truth.

THE CONTRARY EXPERIENCE

I

You cry as the gull cries
dipping low where the tide has ebbed
over the vapid reaches: your impulse
died in the second summer of the war.

The years dip their boughs
brokenly over the uncovered springs.
Hands wasted for love and poetry
finger the hostile gunmetal.

Called to meaningless action
you hesitate
meditating faith to a conscience
more patently noble.

2

But even as you wait
like Arjuna in his chariot
the ancient wisdom whispers:
Live in action.

I do not forget the oath
taken one frosty dawn
when the shadows stretched
from horizon to horizon:

Not to repeat the false act
not to inflict pain:
To suffer, to hope, to build
to analyse the indulgent heart.

Wounds dried like sealing-wax
upon that bond
But time has broken
the proud mind.

No resolve can defeat suffering
no desire establish joy:
Beyond joy and suffering
is the equable heart

not indifferent to glory
if it lead to death
seeking death
if it lead to the only life.

3

Lybia, Egypt, Hellas
the same tide ebbing, the same gull crying
desolate shores and rocky deserts
hunger, thirst, death

the storm threatening and the air still
but other wings
librating in the ominous hush
and the ethereal voice

thrilling and clear.

Buffeted against the storm's sullen breath
the lark rises
over the grey dried grasses
rises and sings.

A WORLD WITHIN A WAR

L'espérance est le seul bien que le dégoût respecte
                                            VAUVENARGUES

I

Sixteen years ago I built this house
By an oak tree on an acre of wild land
Its walls white against the beechwood
Its roof of Norfolk reed and sedge.

The mossy turf I levelled for a lawn
But for the most part left the acre wild
Knowing I could never live
From its stony soil. My work is within
Between three stacks of books. My window
Looks out on a long line of elms.

A secular and insecure retreat—
The alien world is never far away.
Over the ridge, beyond the elms
The railway runs: a passing train
Sends a faint tremor through the ground
Enough to sever a rotted picture-cord

Or rattle the teaspoon against my cup.
A dozen times a day a red bus
Trundles down the lane: there is the screech and scuttle
Of minor traffic: voices rise
Suddenly from silent wheels.
But such dusty veins drain the land
And leave an interstitial stillness.

The hedgehog and the grass-snake
Still haunt my wood. Winter
Brings the starv'd wildings nearer: once
We woke to find a fox's tracks
Printed on the crisp film of snow.
It was the first year of my second war
When every night a madden'd yaffle
Thrummed on the icicled thatch.
Another day a reckless kestrel
Dashed against a gable and fell
Dead at my feet: the children
Watched its dying flutter and the fiery eye
Slowly eclips'd under a dim grey lid.

For years the city like a stream of lava
Crept towards us: now its flow
Is frozen in fear. To the sere earth
The ancient ritual returns: the months
Have their heraldic labours once again.
A tractor chugs through frozen clods
And gold buds bead the gorse
In coppices where besom-heads are cut.
Hedges are trimm'd again and primroses
Bunched in splendour on the open banks.
The sparring rooks pick twigs
For shockhead nests built high
In the dark tracery of the elms.
April and the nightingales will come
From an alien world. The squirrels
Chatter in the green hazel-trees.

The nuthatch inspects the oak's ribb'd bark
While the robin jumps round his own domain.
The hay is mown in June. With summer
Comes all ripeness, rusty, red and gold
To die in September. The reaper
Spirals round the blanch'd fields
The corn diminishing until at last
The expected moment comes and rabbits
Zigzag across the glistening stubble
Pursued by yelping dogs and sudden guns.
In December the corn is thresh'd:
In the frosty evening the engine's smoke
Trails slowly above the berried twigs
And meets the rising mist.

2

Sedate within this palisade
Which unforethinking I have made

Of brittle leaves and velvet flowers,
I re-indite a Book of Hours—

Would emulate the Lombard School
(Crisp as medals, bright but cool)

Talk mainly of the Human Passion
That made us in a conscious fashion

Strive to control our human fate:
But in the margins interpolate

Apes and angels playing tunes
On harpsichords or saxophones

Throughout the story thus maintain
Under a sacred melody the bass profane.

My saints were often silly men
Fond of wine and loose with women.

When they rose to holy stature
They kept the whims of human nature

Were mystics in their London gardens
Or wore instead of hairshirts burdens

Of a mild domestic sort: but so devout
That suddenly they would go out

And die for freedom in the street
Or fall like partridges before a butt

Of ambush'd tyranny and hate.
Other legends will relate

The tale of men whose only love
Was simple work: whose usual lives

Were formed in mirth and music, or in words
Whose golden echoes are wild rewards

For all our suffering, unto death . . .

On the last page a colophon
Would conclude the liberal plan

Showing Man within a frame
Of trophies stolen from a dream.

3

The busy routine kills the flowers
That blossom only on the casual path.
The gift is sacrificed to gain: the gain
Is ploughed into the hungry ground

The best of life is sparely spent
In contemplation of those laws
Illustrious in leaves, in tiny webs
Spun by the ground-spider: in snailshells
And mushroom gills: in acorns and gourds—
The design everywhere evident
The purpose still obscure

                                    In a free hour
I walk through the woods with God
When the air is calm and the midges
Hover in the netted sun and stillness.
Deep then I sink in reverie. There is rest
Above the beating heart: the body
Settles round its axis: mind simulates
The crystal in the cooling rock
The theorem in the beetle's eye—
After the day's mutations
Finds the silver node of sleep. . . .

In that peace
Mind looks into a mirror pois'd
Above body: sees in perspective
Guts, bones and glands: the make of a man.
Out of that labyrinth
The man emerges: becomes
What he is: by no grace
Can become other: can only seize
The pattern in the bone, in branching veins
In clever vesicles and valves
And imitate in acts that beauty.

His nature is God's nature: but torn
How torn and fretted by vain energies
The darting images of eye and ear
Veil'd in the web of memory
Drifts of words that deaden
The subtle manuals of sense.

But the pattern once perceiv'd and held
Is then viable; in good gait and going
In fine song and singular sign: in all
God's festival of perfect form.

4

Here is my cell: here my houselings
Gentle in love, excelling hate, extending
Tokens of friendship to free hearts.

But well we know there is a world without
Of alarm and horror and extreme distress
Where pity is a bond of fear
And only the still heart has grace.
An ancient road winds through the wood
The wood is dark: a chancel where the mind
Sways in terror of the formal foe.

Their feet upon the peat and sand
Made no sound. But sounds were everywhere around
Life rustled under fallen leaves, rotted twigs
Snapped like rafters above the heads
Of those friars preachers, constant and firm
Who in charity advanced against the Arian hate
Ambush'd against them. See now
The falchion falls: the martyr's limbs
Lie like trimm'd branches on the ground.

    The ancient road winds through the wood
    A path obscure and frail.

    The martyr takes it and the man
    Who makes the martyr by his deed.

    Death waits on evil and on holiness
    Death waits in the leafy labyrinth.
    There is a grace to still the blood
    Of those who take the daring path:

172

There is a grace that fills the dying eye
With pity for the wielder of the axe.

There is a grace that nulls the pain
Of martyrs in their hour of death.

Death is no pain to desperate men.

Vision itself is desperate: the act
Is born of the ideal: the hand
Must seize the hovering grail.

The sense of glory stirs the heart
Out of its stillness: a white light
Is in the hills and the thin cry
Of a hunter's horn. We shall act
We shall build
A crystal city in the age of peace
Setting out from an island of calm
A limpid source of love.

5

The branches break. The beaters
Are moving in: lie still my loves
Like deer: let the lynx
Glide through the dappled underwoods.
Lie still: he cannot hear: he may not see.

Should the ravening death descend
We will be calm: die like the mouse
Terrified but tender. The claw
Will meet no satisfaction in our sweet flesh
And we shall have known peace

In a house beneath a beechwood
In an acre of wild land.

THE HEART CONSCRIPTED

The shock of silver tassels
the sledded breath . . .
I who have fought my battles
keep these in a sheath.

The ulcer of exact remorse
from which the Lake poet perished,
the owl's indifferent hood—
these have vanished.

I hear only the sobbing fall
of various water-clocks
and the swift inveterate wail
of the destructive axe.

Lorca was killed, singing,
and Fox who was my friend.
The rhythm returns: the song
which has no end.

THE THIRD

We two that live together
And love each other
Have no wandering thoughts
Beyond the present measure.

We love and work and subtly weave
Habitual chains: we wheel
Like birds above our focal hearth
Our fear-fring'd nest.

But always breaking through the screen
Of silence comes the warning note:

The world is not within us, we
In part are in some way without.

Peeping into our private room
We feel, not see, a Third:
The hollyhocks are parted and a face
Presses to the window and is gone.

Fine fingers I have felt
Like icy bands about my arms
Just when the impulse had been born
To demonstrate my tenderness.

The Person or the Thing has age
But is indefinite:
I would not care if I could force
Its sullen hand

And see an instrument of hate
Fall clattering to the ground
Or know that all it held was death
The Third to which we both are bound.

With death one day I shall pledge faith
And faithless be to you:
But who is this that treads between
The last bed and our own?

Is it the wind in the hollyhocks?
A trickle of cloud and glass?
A nerve discordant round the bone?
A simple weariness?

Dear, do not let us hesitate
To shun the unbidden guest:
Resolv'd that all is distortion
Save life, and love, and death.

175

THE IVY AND THE ASH

The ivy and the ash
cast a dark arm
across the beck.
In this rocky ghyll
I sit and watch
the eye-iris water move
like muscles over stones
smooth'd by this ageless action.

The water brings
from the high fell
an icy current of air.
There is no sun to splinter
the grey visionary quartz.
The heart is cool
and adamant among the rocks
mottled with wet moss.

Descend into the valley
explore the plain
even the salt sea
but keep the heart
cool in the memory
of ivy, ash
and the glistening beck
running swiftly through the black rocks.

KIRKDALE

I, Orm the son of Gamal
found these fractur'd stones
starting out of the fragrant thicket.
The river bed was dry.

The rooftrees naked and bleach'd.
nettles in the nave and aisleways,
on the altarstone an owl's cast
and a feather from a wild dove's wing.

There was peace in the valley:
far into the eastern sea
the foe had gone, leaving death and ruin
and a longing for the priest's solace.

Fast the feather lay
like a sulky jewel in my head
till I knew it had fallen in a holy place.
Therefore I raised these grey stones up again.

THE LABYRINTH

Unicume has come in from the cowshed
with a lantern that still burns bright:
His enormous shadow
staggers round the white room.

The moist sweet smell of birth
clings to him like vapour to the harsh earth
His arms in that house asleep
might be sever'd from his heart.

In the shed he has left
a beast that licks its newborn calf:
Entrails which were once embryonic
coil into his weary brain

And the lines on his unwounded brow
are beaded with blood.

EMBLEM

In measure and in marksmanship
   lies the exactitude of death:
Through the neat red wound on the pale brow
   the bullet has driven a path.

With calliper and compass
   and a straight divided rule
The Arab made the rose a rosette
   to prove himself a fool.

Beauty has no other reason
   than the eye can indicate;
Only the miraculous conception
   is immaculate.

FELIX TRANSITUS

The valley and the crest
the heavy lid of night
the arch of bone
a head which on the breast
has fallen like a kite
wind-driven down.

The darkness of the earth
the sense of sinking deep
the blatant heart.
This stillness might be death
it is not sleep
it does not hurt.

An intercepted edge of lace
has printed on his brow
its faultless mcsh;
and blood has left a trace
where lips unconscious now
once bruised the flesh.

COLLECTED POEMS
(1946, 1953)

EXILE'S LAMENT

Here where I labour hour by hour
The folk are mean and land is sour.

God grant I may return to die
Between the Riccall and the Rye.

1945

They came running over the perilous sands
   Children with their golden eyes
Crying: *Look! We have found samphire*
   Holding out their bone-ridden hands.

It might have been the spittle of wrens
   Or the silver nest of a squirrel
For I was invested with the darkness
   Of an ancient quarrel whose omens
Lay scatter'd on the silted beach.
   The children came running toward me

But I saw only the waves behind them
   Cold, salt and disastrous
Lift their black banners and break
   Endlessly, without resurrection.

MOON'S FARM AND POEMS MOSTLY ELEGIAC (1955)

MOON'S FARM

A Dialogue for Three Voices

A cave in the old quarry
a dry ditch and a tumbledown barn
such is all my shelter.
The black-faced sheep have gone
and with them the shepherds . . .
That was twenty winters ago.
Then came the men with axes
cut down the spinneys and plantations
lopped off the branches
   and carted the timber away
leaving this desolation
   at the head of the dale.

Oh, I can nestle in a ferny glen
or in the rafters of a fallen roof
   in myrtle bushes at the edge of the bog
But I grow weak
   I have no nourishment
      I languish like a mist at noon.

Once it was different.
That was in the time of the holy men
monks who came over the moor
   from the abbey by the sea
to build a monastery in the slender woods
   at the dale's mouth.
Their path
led up the dale and across the hills
and on the hills they had many sheep
and cattle in the meadows below the hills

187

They dammed up the beck
   to make fishponds
and ran off a sluice
   to drive the millwheel.

They cared for me
and built me in with woods and garths
   with farmsteads and sheepfolds
     with chapels and graveyards
even their dead
   they gave to me.
Now the broken stones of their buildings
   lie under these grassy mounds and heather
I am left
   with birds and beetles for company
     and the little grey snails in the turf
Even the foxes and badgers
   have left this place
There is no strength at all
   left in the place.

SECOND VOICE

About here it must have been
   but there is nothing left
     nothing left of Moon's Farm.
There was a clump of pines
   the last trees before the heather began
And a stone trough
   to gather the clear water from a rill
It fell from a stone spout which must have been very old
   fifty years ago they had given up carving such things
     from the solid stone
     (took too much time, they said)
Time, time
   folk were already beginning to be aware of time
     even then.

Not aware enough!
When you live all the time in the same place
Then you become aware of time.

I begin to remember everything
   but how it has changed!
There were woods on the other side of the dale
   and down there
      by the beck
was Moon's Farm.
Not a stone or stick of it left!
That's a mystery—
   how completely a solid structure
      like a farmhouse
can vanish in fifty years!
The stones they would carry off
   to make a new road
      miles away
But what happened to the trees?
   there was even a stunted orchard
All gone.
All signs of human habitation
rubbed off the landscape.
And yet
   there is still something. I still feel
      the spirit of the place.

He is becoming aware of me.

It was made up of so many things:
the shapes of these hills
   and the changing shadows

the cries of birds
   and the lapping of the stream over pebbles.
But more than that—
   a sense of glory and yes
     a sense of grief.
Glory in the present moment
Grief because it was all so momentary
   so fleeting
     so elusive.
And yet I am sure
   it was more than an illusion
some spirit did inhabit these hills
   some very ancient spirit.
The Roman legions passed this way
   the stones of their roads lie under the heather
Did they salute her as they passed?
But there you are
   already personifying the thing
     imagining some wispy female.
The Romans were not so sentimental
their genius loci was masculine
   the devil of a fellow.
Hullo!
   there's someone coming up from the beck
   looks like an old beggar woman
     but what would she find up here?
She must have seen me from the other side
   and now comes to investigate.
But she takes her time.

FIRST VOICE

Now he has seen me.
He is walking into my world with his innocent eyes
He is looking straight into my hiding-place.

SECOND VOICE

Good morning!
I did not expect to meet anybody up here. You surely
   don't live hereabouts.

FIRST VOICE

Indeed I do. I have always
   lived in this dale.

SECOND VOICE

Then perhaps you can help me. I too
   used to live in this dale
      but farther down.
I left fifty years ago
   as a boy of ten
I went far away
   into another country.
Today, for the first time
I have come back.
I find everything changed.

FIRST VOICE

Oh yes: it has changed a lot
   in that long time.

SECOND VOICE

It is partly an illusion
   or *was* an illusion.
You see: everything, yes, every thing
   is much smaller than I can remember.
My childish eyes
   had magnified everything
and now the world seems to have shrunk.

FIRST VOICE

When your possessions are small
  you enlarge them with wonder.
My world
  remains always the same

SECOND VOICE

You speak like an educated woman
  yet you say
    you have never left the dale.

FIRST VOICE

I have never left the dale: my schooling
  was indeed simple.

SECOND VOICE

But apparently profound.
I went to many schools
  and was no wiser in the end.
I did not know, for example,
  that this dale would shrink.
I thought I should find it
  as I had left it
    the people changed, of course
      most of them dead
        many gone away
but I thought the place would be the same.

FIRST VOICE

It changes slowly.
The trees are felled
  or brought down in a storm
and no one plants new ones.

The roofs fall in
   the stones crumble
      men go away in search of easier work.
Only the hills
   remain
      in their old shape.

SECOND VOICE

And why have you been left behind
   apparently alone?

FIRST VOICE

I am not alone.
I have a Father.

SECOND VOICE

A Father! And how old is he?

FIRST VOICE

You must ask him—I don't know.

SECOND VOICE

Is he about?

FIRST VOICE

Yes: he is always about.
You will see him presently.

SECOND VOICE

Good! Are there any more in the family?

FIRST VOICE

That depends
  on what you mean by a family.
Sometimes
  we have people to stay with us.

SECOND VOICE

For a holiday, no doubt.

FIRST VOICE

From time to time.

SECOND VOICE

Now I can see your Father
  he is coming down the hillside.
But the sun is in his eyes
  he does not see us.

FIRST VOICE

Oh yes: he sees everything
he can stare the sun out
he can see in the dark.

SECOND VOICE

How extraordinary! You mean . . .

FIRST VOICE

Hush! About such things
  he must tell you himself.

194

THIRD VOICE

Ah! I thought I would catch up with you here.

SECOND VOICE

But I came
   from the opposite direction.

THIRD VOICE

Yes: but I came to meet you.

SECOND VOICE

But I don't understand . . .

THIRD VOICE

Never mind! The point is
What are you going to do next?

FIRST VOICE

He means
Where are you going to next?

SECOND VOICE

Does it matter to you?
I am not trespassing, am I?

FIRST VOICE

You are not trespassing
If you stay here.

THIRD VOICE

You surely have time enough.

SECOND VOICE

You mean
you would like me to stay with you?

FIRST AND THIRD VOICES

For as long as you like.

FIRST VOICE

You would gradually recover
    the feeling of the place.

THIRD VOICE

You would gradually recover
    the sense of the past.

SECOND VOICE

Ah, that's just what I came for.
I will gladly stay. I have the few necessary things
    in that rucksack.

FIRST VOICE

I will go to prepare a bed for you.
I am afraid it will be a very simple one
    we have no house.

SECOND VOICE

It is very kind of you
    anything will do.

THIRD VOICE

We are what you would call tramps.

SECOND VOICE

Yes: but I don't see
what you can possibly find to live on
    in a place like this.

THIRD VOICE

One needs less and less
    after a certain age.

SECOND VOICE

Yes: that is what I am beginning to discover.

THIRD VOICE

Until one needs nothing at all.

SECOND VOICE

You mean
    we die.

THIRD VOICE

That's right
    you will die.

SECOND VOICE

Tell me: were you too
  here fifty years ago?

THIRD VOICE

Yes, of course.

SECOND VOICE

You don't remember me, I suppose?

THIRD VOICE

I remember you perfectly well
  the boy at the Scarlets.

SECOND VOICE

Yes: that was the name of our farm.
But surely
you cannot recognize in my wasted features
  the boy of fifty years ago?

THIRD VOICE

There are some things that do not change
  the shape of the skull
  the cadence of the voice.

SECOND VOICE

But if you remember me so well
why don't I remember you?
I would say
  I had never seen you before.

THIRD VOICE

No: in those days
   you were not aware of me.

SECOND VOICE

So we might say
you have the advantage over me.

THIRD VOICE

So we might say. But you will not forget me
ever again.

SECOND VOICE

It's not likely. Meeting you like this
   in this lonely place.
Can you tell me what the time is?
   it must be getting late . . .

(*A shrill scream*)

What was that?

THIRD VOICE

A rabbit—perhaps, if we are lucky, a hare.
It is all we have to live on
   up here.

SECOND VOICE

I have heard wounded men scream like that.
But I was asking you the time . . .

199

THIRD VOICE

I can still see you
   the day you nearly lost your life
     in the mill-dam.

SECOND VOICE

You were there!

THIRD VOICE

Yes: standing on the far bank
   watching the water-rats
I saw how you were pulled out
   as good as dead.

SECOND VOICE

No wonder I didn't see you!
And shortly after that narrow squeak
   I went away.
That is why there was never any chance
   of getting to know you.
You stayed in the dale
   I never came back
     until today.

THIRD VOICE

I stayed here.

SECOND VOICE

And perhaps that was wise of you. I wonder
I wonder what I would have done
   had I stayed here
what would I have become.

THIRD VOICE

We can only become what we are.

SECOND VOICE

True enough—'Become what thou art!'—an oracle
I have always believed in.

THIRD VOICE

So it made no difference
   going away?

SECOND VOICE

No essential difference, I suppose. And yet
   it is said we only learn by experience.

THIRD VOICE

And what did experience teach you?

SECOND VOICE

To discover myself
   perhaps only that.

THIRD VOICE

And other people?

SECOND VOICE

They remained mysteries
   except in so far as I got
      inside their skulls
And even then
   it was pretty dark inside.

THIRD VOICE

But how did you discover yourself?

SECOND VOICE

Curiously enough
    in exploring other people.
I didn't discover that I was a male
    until I had known a female
I did not discover that I was an Englishman
    until I fought with a German
I did not discover that I was a European
    until I had lived in America.
Shall I go on?

THIRD VOICE

Yes: to the end.

SECOND VOICE

It has no end—yet.
I did not discover that I was alone in the world
    until I joined an army
I did not discover that I was brave
    until I had sheltered in a ditch with a coward
I did not discover that I was a liar
    until I met a man who never lied
        even to save his pride
I did not discover that I was sober
    until one night I got dead drunk
I did not discover that I could hate
    until I fell in love.
A mass of contradictions
    you will say.

THIRD VOICE

There is no unity in human character
Only God and the Devil are consistent.
But go on.

SECOND VOICE

I did not discover that I was a peasant
    until I became a poet
I did not discover that I was miserly
    until I became rich
I did not discover that I was strong
    until God had forsaken me.

THIRD VOICE

Until you had forsaken God.

SECOND VOICE

No : it did not happen like that
I did not deliberately forsake God.
Rather I clung to Him
    like a child to its mother's skirts.
But the garment was whisked away
    I fell to the ground.

THIRD VOICE

It may have been
God wanted you to stand alone.

SECOND VOICE

Alone? I have been alone
    all these years.

At first I was proud to be alone
I found I could stand without a hand
    clutching at the finger of God
I was defiant and cried: God is dead.
But then
    I grew less certain
It was not that I believed in a resurrection of the dead God.
But it became obvious
    that for some people he was still alive.
I could not convince them that he was dead
    and when they looked at me
        it was with eyes of pity
            as for someone who had lost a father or a son.
I scorned their pity
    but I no longer despised their belief.

THIRD VOICE

You did not try
    to find your lost God?

SECOND VOICE

No. If God is still alive
    he is with us now
staring us in the face
His face is the sky
His eyes are red berries in yon hedge
    or the glittering quartz in this stone.
His voice is that bird
    crying in the gorse bush
    or the water
        lapping over the pebbles in the beck.
If God exists
    he must be both immanent and ubiquitous
What sort of God would play hide-and-seek?

THIRD VOICE

It takes two to play such a game.

SECOND VOICE

Yes: man is just as necessary to God
    as God to man.
God depends for his existence
    on our recognition of Him.
God is reborn
    in every woman's womb.

THIRD VOICE

God exists but for a moment.

SECOND VOICE

The moment of our attention—or do you mean
that time will still exist
    when God is dead?

THIRD VOICE

That is what I mean.

SECOND VOICE

You are a very strange old man
    to talk so confidently
        about God and Fate.
I did not expect to find a man like you
    in such a lonely place.

THIRD VOICE

In such a lonely place
no man would stay
who had not made his peace
   with the eyes in the berries
     and the voice in the beck.

SECOND VOICE

Yes: most of us ignore them
   run away from them
     and think we have escaped
       their obstinate questionings.
Oh, I too ran away from them
   and have managed fairly well to forget them!
And that is how we begin to deceive ourselves
that, at any rate, is how I
   began to deceive myself
     began to 'avoid the issue' as we say . . .
Avoid the issue!
To be honest I ought to say
     that that is how I began to practise hypocrisy . . .
Hypocrisy
   is perhaps rather a strong word for it
Let me call it dissimulation
I had a habit
   no, not a habit—an innate disposition
to identify myself with the other person.
Sometimes it worked
   and sometimes it didn't.
I could not identify myself with very poor people
   nor with very rich people
     their upbringings had been so different.
But if a Christian began to talk to me
   assuming that I was a Christian
     I did not disabuse him

or if an aggressive patriot began to talk to me
    assuming that I would be willing to destroy a whole city
      with a single bomb
again I did not disabuse him.
It was not cowardice—on some other occasion
I would freely express
    an unorthodox opinion.
It may sometimes have been indolence—what I call
    my lazy larynx
      (for I have always felt
        the effort of talking).
Such is my physical disposition . . .
Voices
    how they expose us
      how they form our thoughts
A man's mind
    is an echo of his voice—or rather
      of his voices.

THIRD VOICE

Voices?

SECOND VOICE

Yes: we have two voices
    the instinctive voice that flows like water from a spring
      or blood from a wound
    and the intellectual voice that blares like a fanfare
      from some centre in the brain.

THIRD VOICE

I have only one voice
    but it is new every day.

Like the sun. But the ancient man who said
   that the sun was new every day
had spent his life seeking himself.
But the same ancient man said
   that though you travel in every direction
     you will never find the boundaries of the self
      so deep is the logos of it.
And that is the truth I have discovered. In the end
   I came back here
     to the scene of my birth and infancy.
I thought I might find the truth about myself here
but I don't see the end of my search yet!
So deep is the logos!

THIRD VOICE

The logos? Now that
   is not a word we use here.

SECOND VOICE

If I could tell you what such a word means
   I should be at the end of my task!
It is the most mysterious word
   in the history of human thought.
'In the beginning was the Word
   and the Word was with God
     and the Word was God'. . .
I began to puzzle over that sentence
   when I was still a child
and I think most Christians have wondered
   why such a strange ambiguous word
     Word itself
should stand at the beginning of their Gospel.
Perhaps it is because the word

is the only link that exists between the known and the
                                                unknown
    between man and the cosmos.
If man had not been able to utter the word of God
    he would never have conceived the idea of God
And so God was first manifested to man in speech
    and in the poetry inherent in speech
        in the logos.
That is perhaps fairly obvious
but the more I have pondered on this fact
    the more I have realized the predicament into which we
        as men
are thrown by this dependence on logos.
For two things could happen
    and did happen.
In the beginning there was the cosmos
    (or nature as we more politely call it)
and in the midst of the cosmos
    and part of it
        was man
            growing aware of his environment.
He slowly perfected words to express his predicament.
But then the word became God
the instrument that had enabled man to express the idea of
                                            an outer cosmos
    was identified with the idea to be expressed.
Men then worshipped
    not the cosmos of which they were a part
        but the idea of the cosmos which they could
                            separate from themselves as a word
and make absolute as an idea.
But that was not the end.
Eventually
    and not so long ago
man conceived the notion that his kind
in inventing the word
    the logos
had invented God.

o   209

The idea of God
   had not risen from man's experience of the world
      but had been an original intuition of the mind
         an idea divinely inspired
            a glimpse of some transcendental realm of being
where time does not exist.

THIRD VOICE

I cannot conceive of such a realm.

SECOND VOICE

Nor I.
I have always felt perfectly satisfied
   with a natural outlook on life.
By this I do not mean
   the outlook of what is called natural science.
Materialists of that kind
   stand this side of the logos.
They assume
   that their words and signs are fixed and measurable
                               entities
   that with their words and signs
      they can explain the cosmos.
That is childish
   or perverse.
But it is merely a higher childishness
   to go to the opposite extreme
      that is to say
         beyond the natural function of the logos
to assume the autonomous reality
   of a realm with which we cannot communicate
      except by means of the logos.
In the beginning was the word
   and in the end are many words
      nets to catch the butterfly truth.

THIRD VOICE

Truth! so that is what you are looking for!
You thought you would find the truth up here?

SECOND VOICE

I'm sorry—truth
is a word I did not mean to bring into our conversation
    it is an evil word I have sworn not to use.
Truth
    is that for which men kill each other.
I limit my search to myself
I know that my self is different from all other selves
    and that what I discover
        is not going to be the envy of anyone else.

THIRD VOICE

But if you discover the truth
    you will be the envy of the world.
You must therefore avoid the truth
    even the truth about yourself.

SECOND VOICE

Well, if I do discover the truth about myself
I must keep it to myself.
    It will be my secret.

THIRD VOICE

What is the good of a secret
    known only to yourself?

SECOND VOICE

Perhaps I should say
   the secret of my strength
   strength is the knowledge of one's limits
    and that knowledge
      helps a man to endure his fate.
The man that knows himself
   can almost foresee his fate.

THIRD VOICE

Is that any consolation?

SECOND VOICE

Consolation?—not exactly.
But it gives to life
   the excitement of a game of chance.
There a man goes
   spinning out the thread of his destiny
    millions more are doing the same thing.
The threads cross
   and turn
    and cross again
and the pattern that emerges we call history.
A crazy pattern
   but the only one that exists. . . .

THIRD VOICE

And when the thread is cut?

SECOND VOICE

Why, then the pattern changes
but so infinitely little
   it makes no difference.

THIRD VOICE

But the thread is your individual life:
it makes a difference to you.

SECOND VOICE

Not so long as I remain
aware of the beauty of the pattern.

THIRD VOICE

You are sitting on the edge of the moor.
Beyond the moor is the sea
   the unknown
We are standing on the edge of the world
   and what do we see
     as we look over the edge?

SECOND VOICE

Our human eyes see very little
   the stars and the planets
worlds beyond worlds
   universe without end.

THIRD VOICE

You don't know
   that it is without end.

SECOND VOICE

I know nothing
   beyond what my eyes
     or my eyes aided by clever instruments
tell me.
I can guess a little.

THIRD VOICE

Yes, but at the end of your guessing
   what do you see?

SECOND VOICE

Nothing
I cannot see anything beyond the evidence of my senses.
There may be something
   an unending Thing
   Nothing or Something
I do not know.

THIRD VOICE

And you do not fear
   anything?

SECOND VOICE

Fear? Why should I be afraid?

THIRD VOICE

You are not afraid of the unknown?

SECOND VOICE

I do not think the unknown is a subject
   to inspire one with feelings of any kind.
Before such an unconceivable concept
   my mind is merely blank.

THIRD VOICE

Blank?
Have you then no curiosity?

Of course—unending, restless, curiosity.
But my curiosity
   nibbles away at the edge of the known
   it does not take a leap into nothingness.
It looks back at the wide and solid expanse of the known
   looks back
      and is lost in wonder.

THIRD VOICE

Wonder?

SECOND VOICE

That is another of my pet words. Wonder
   is the antidote to fear
   the essence of courage.
We say we are lost in wonder
   as though it were a forest
      or a sea.
But wonder invades us like the warmth of the sun.
Our very consciousness expands when we discover
   some corner of the pattern of the universe
      realize its endless implications
      and know ourselves
         to be part of that intricate design.

THIRD VOICE

But surely that discovery
   is the beginning of humility?

SECOND VOICE

No: humility is for human relationships
   an attitude of man to man.

215

But when I discover the same geometrical proportions
   in the human body and in a flower
     or a crystal
   in a cathedral
   and in a planetary system
then I am not humble.
Nor am I proud, for it is no effort of man
   that has created such correspondencies.
I am excited by such a thought
perhaps my heart beats more quickly
   or my eyes dilate
     for I am filled with wonder.

THIRD VOICE

But the day will come
   when your heart will stop beating
and your eyes will no longer
   be aware of any of these wonders.

SECOND VOICE

Yet death
   is the greatest wonder of all.
That life can be extinguished
   is a fact as wonderful as the fact
     that it can be conceived.
The chance that you or I
   or any particular person
is born
   is an infinite one
and with the thought of the infinitude of that chance
   we should be ready to accept
     the finiteness of death. It is
       simply
our fate.

You did not hear me return
  but I have been standing behind you
    listening.
Your bed is ready.

SECOND VOICE

Thank you: I will come along presently. You were kind
  to listen patiently to all this nonsense.

FIRST VOICE

I did not mean to interrupt
  but I thought you had finished.

THIRD VOICE

It was the word Fate
  that made us pensive.

SECOND VOICE

It is a word that seems to end all argument.
There is no appeal against fate
  and no sense in discussing it.

THIRD VOICE

Not if you imagine it as an enemy. But it isn't!
It has been said
  man's character is his fate.

FIRST VOICE

Man is more than his fate.
Man is moulded in a womb
  and dissolved in earth
His foundations are two tombs
He is like earth uprisen.

SECOND VOICE

I think I agree. A character can be uprooted.
We are proud
   of our upright posture
   of our legs that can carry us out of this dale
      into the wide world.
Men are proud of the machines that carry them over the seas
   through the air.
But they carry their character with them
   and their character is their destiny.
But
   our characters are sometimes seduced.
If I am sitting in an aeroplane above the Atlantic
I have surrendered my fate to the pilot of the plane.
It might be said
   only a man of my character would fly across the Atlantic
but the same anonymous chances
   follow me on land and by sea.
It is not in man's character to desert his home—
That is what one calls
   tempting Fate
and tempting Fate does not mean
   that we act as if we accept our fate
it means acting in defiance of our fate.
I do not mean
   that restlessness cannot be our fate.
Man was once a nomadic animal
   and traces of the nomad
      linger in his groins.
But we have perfected ourselves in stillness.

FIRST VOICE

In suffering and in joy.

SECOND VOICE

Yes: I meant to imply suffering and joy.
Fate is not ameliorative.

But who can separate
   beauty and terror
      suffering and joy?
I remember a valley in Greece.
I came to it
   when the light was failing.
The rocky hills were purple
   the sky a thin icy green
      fading eastward to a slatey grey.
There was a huge mound, partly excavated
   to reveal colossal stones
      the foundations of a fortress.
In the hillside was a tomb
   the tomb of a legendary king
      faultlessly shaped and tense
      like the inside of an eggshell.
I viewed it by the light
   of a fire of withered thyme . . .
When I emerged
   it was dark in the valley and I felt around me
      the nameless terror that had penetrated the lives of that
                                      ancient king
        his adulterous queen
           and all their melancholy issue.
Their fates had overtaken them
   in that place
      more than three thousand years ago
and man had not dared to build again
   not on such a site of horror.
But I knew then
   that man's fate is not like a seed
   carried hither and thither by the wind
not like spawn on a restless tide
But is the creation of generations of men
   men who have lived in one place
      and absorbed its mysteries.

Mysteries?

Perhaps there are no mysteries of time or place
but there are mysteries of life.
A mystery
    is what is hidden, and it is Life
    not God
        that loves to hide.
It is Life
        not God
        that is mysterious.
The Greeks were right again: it is Life
    that plays the game of hide-and-seek
The rhythm of the seasons
    is the interplay of Life and Death. In the person of
                                        Persephone
    it is Life itself
        that disappears for a wintry season.
But hiding involves a hiding-place. In Eleusis
    you can still see the pit
    down which Persephone sank
        to Pluto's dark realm.
All the ancient myths
    are precisely located. And today we have no myths
because we have no sense of place.
Our beliefs
    are like untethered balloons
    they drift into the clouds
        into the transcendental inane.
I would sooner men worshipped a tree or a rock.

And yourself
    what have you worshipped?

Ah! you have some right
  to ask me that question
    for it embarrasses me.
The truth is
  I have never been able to worship anything
    not even myself.
Worship is an act of adoration
  the complete surrender of the self to some Other
    to some Otherness.
It must be a great relief
  to get rid of that burden sometimes
    to feel utterly empty
      like a room that has been swept and made bright
        ready for a new occupant
to return to a body that has been renewed in ecstasy!
It is an illusion, of course
  but one of the desirable illusions.

Have you then lived without illusions?

Never for a moment.
I have lived with the illusion
  that I was in love
with the illusion
  that my loved ones loved me
with the illusion
  that I could give happiness to other people
    as you would give a rose to a young girl
with the illusion
  that other people would see the world with my eyes
    and love the things that I love

with the illusion
    that my words would open men's hearts
        and give them understanding.
For fifty years I have lived
    in successive states of illusion
        and I am still not completely
disillusioned.

THIRD VOICE

What illusions remain to you?

SECOND VOICE

The illusion that it is not yet too late
    for any of these illusions to be re-established.
The illusion
    that a voice in the wilderness echoes in some green valley
the illusion that the wind
    or a bird
will take up the seed I have scattered on stony ground
    and drop it in a fertile field
the illusion
    that bitterness is dissolved in the serenity of old age
the illusion
    that I shall die a happy man.

THIRD VOICE

And at the time of your death
what could make you happy?

SECOND VOICE

To die without fear and trembling.

THIRD VOICE

You are describing a state of happiness. You do not tell us
    what would ensure such a state.

I am not sure that I know.
I suppose at the end I shall come to another Place
   it might be this dale-head
   it might be my white bedroom
   it might be a busy street.
I might die in pain
   in weariness
      or in despair.
But if at the last moment
I could see some perfect form
   it might be this fern at my feet
   or a sparrow flickering past my window
   or a painting on the wall
   or some poet's vision of eternity
     like a great Ring of pure and endless Light
     all calm, as it was bright . . .
Granted that I could at the last moment
see some bright image
   I should die without fear and trembling.
It is when we look into the abyss of nothingness
   infinite nothingness
that we lose courage
   and die swearing
     or die praying.

FIRST VOICE

Yes: men should hold on to tangible things.
Stay with me in these hills and glens
where the birds cry lovingly to their young
   and the waters are never silent.

THIRD VOICE

Die to the day and its trivialities
Die to the sense of time.

FIRST VOICE

Or to the sense of place
to the place of generation and birth.

THIRD VOICE

Live with the sun by day and with the stars by night.

FIRST VOICE

Live with your eyes and ears
    and the exercise of your subtle fingers.

THIRD VOICE

Live in the moment of attention.

FIRST VOICE

Live in the presence of things.

(A silence)

SECOND VOICE

It is getting dark.
I can hardly see you.

FIRST VOICE

Yes: it is dark now.
I shall lead you to your bed.

SECOND VOICE

You said it was down by the beck, didn't you?

It is not far.

And the way up and the way down are the same.
I go up the hill.

My Father will be with us again tomorrow.

As boys we used to come here
    to gather wild daffodils.
At Moon's Farm the pump was in the kitchen
    a well of clean crystal water.
And there was an old clock
    standing opposite the kitchen door.
It had a robin
    or perhaps it was a wren
painted on its white face
    but the fingers never moved
It was always 12.25 at Moon's Farm.
12.25 is God's time.

THE DEATH OF KROPOTKIN

Emma said there had been snow
and a cold wind sighing in the wither'd branches
I imagined trivial details
sheepswool caught in the thorns
red berries
and a prophet's dead face on the pillow.

She said he had died in peace
and the eternal intelligence on his brow
had seemed like a light
in the dark unlit hut.
I imagined
his steel-rimmed glasses on the side-table
and a book abandoned.

She said there had been a great concourse of people
walking out from Moscow
or from the nearest station
poor humble people—Lenin had let them come
to sidle lovingly past
his silent form.

Several hundred people, simple people
fur caps down to their ears
padded trousers criss-crossed with string
standing there on the obliterated road
waiting for the cortège.

Dmitrov was the name of the place.
They took his body to Moscow
and there formed a procession
perhaps a mile long
old revolutionaries, young students
and children carrying wreaths
of holly and laurel.

226

They marched five miles
carrying the black and scarlet banners.
The feathery snow was falling
gently on his bier
gently on the bowed heads
and the patient streets.

But when they reached the burial place
the snow had ceased
and the winter sun
sinking red
stained the level glittering plain.

A river of glowing light
poured into the open grave
all the light in the world
sank with his coffin
into the Russian earth.

It was seven versts outside Moscow.
On the steps of their museum
the Tolstoyans had gathered
to play mournful music
as the cortège passed.

It was dark then and silent.
I remembered, said Emma, the cairn he had found
on the last mountain ridge
a heap of stones and broken branches
with tokens attached of horsehair or rag
and the cry: 'The waters before us
flow now to the Amur.
No mountains more to cross!'

No mountains more to cross
dear comrade and pioneer.
You have crossed the Great Khinghán
travelling eastward into rich lands
where many will follow you.

A GIFT FOR SCARDANELLI

See: the field is empty . . .
You came here by a curious detour
the hedges were trimmed but o-
ranges among the intricate thorns
glowed like torches. You expected to find
a temple of honey-coloured stone
and an old man crouched in the porch
listening to a marble-browed girl
that there discourses on the nature of love.

April und Mai und Junius sind ferne
Ich bin nichts mehr : ich lebe nicht mehr gerne . . .

The clouds are unanchored: they might
fall from the sky to cover you
I have brought you a basket of figs
and some fine linen
but alas
no white goat to slaughter
and fingers have faltered
that should have played the flute.

CAROL

Until I wander'd through the world
   I did not know
That even in Bethlehem
   Falls the white soft snow.

Then I did imagine how
   A morning long ago
Reflected light from all the land
   Flooded through the door

And lit the spidery rafters
  Above the sleeping child
Whose eyes were lifted up to
  A mother mild.

And such a radiance was around
  On ass and munching cow
Some said because a child was born
  And some because of snow.

THE WELL OF LIFE

The waters of the well of life
Lie deep on a rock bed
Not fetched from running streams
But drawn at the well-head.

Two red-haired wives stand there
(Each has a lover)
One turns the wailing windlass
The other bends over

And dips a scoop into the well
To fill the pitcher at her side
The clouds are ghostly passengers
That on the stilled water ride.

The rooks are croaking in the elms
And men in the field labour
God bless these wives and their strong
Men's endeavour.

KALAMIS AND SOSANDRA

Above the lake the swallows dive
And fishes mock their flight:
Who is the goddess gave you birth
On some past starlit night?
Who cut the secret knot of life
And left a hollow where
The lion with the wounded paw
Impressed a seal of air
Invisible yet viable
The seed of my despair
That soon will sprout and climb and cling
Your ivy in my silver hair.

I do not wish another thing
But that you wear no new disguise
You have the wisdom of the young
And I the false youth of the wise
You hold a stylus in your hand
You have placed me on a pedestal
You have carved the torso and the head
Your gaze is on the genital.
A warm breeze blows across the lake
It is the season of the grape
The god the lion and the man
They have a single shape.

SAPPHO

Gently she climbs
the Sicilian steps: leans over the white arch
and now the lenses of her eyes
    have caught
the concentrated golden fire
pouring from the abrupt reflections
    of barbaric walls.

Confidently she will carry
    these essential glories
        these trophies from the well-head
    her conquest absolute.

She can survive the unholy glare
with her fourfold accents of persuasion
    and her hand
out of the electric air will elicit
lyric analogues of the rocky kingdom
    where Minos once
        fed virgins to a spectral maw.

Who can resist
    her gentle grace?

SAPPHO AND ATTHIS

I

We lay upon the Chian isle
    The dark hours through
And heard the impatient waters beat
    Upon the broken shore.

The storm that in its brutal grasp
  A day ago
Clutch'd and compress'd our stricken hearts
  Has left no sign of wrath.

2

I watch the light seep through the clouds
  And sun establish day:
The hills across the bay drink in
  The liquid edge of night.

The fishers come in from the sea
  And now unfold their nets:
I wish that their hands could unravel
  Our intricate mesh.

MYCENE

Time's filial beast
To make his mockery of life
Planted the pale cyclamen aridly: here
Where the nosing goat
Presses an indifferent hoof.

If I might have spoken
I would have said: Pride has no power
To sever the fiery knot
That gathers within the blue stain
Of eyes that might be trembling waters
Were lust to be provoked. I saw you then
Iphigenia or some legendary girl
Crouched over a fire of withered thyme
In Agamemnon's tomb. The flames
Were brief: and left a darkness
Deeper than the night: into which we walked
Strangers to our separate doom.

232

THE STAG

Seven are the forests where he ranges
Browsing the scant oriels of herbage
If he has a haste he has no fear
There is no panther to ravage
The mystical solitude of the oaks.

Maugre the antlers that impede his flight
He advances with indiffident step
Hoary perspectives
Meet and dissolve in his punctual eye.

He will rest where the waters break
Into a white and moist cascade
Frail are the blossoms there
In that perpetual shade.

DEATH OF A GREEK MERCENARY

He had made no history: no song
but seven times he reiterated
as over fragrant bread
the one word *Om*

There was a golden avalanche in the air
of honeysuckle and crumbling stone
the lizards ran invisibly
over a wall that was gone

The startled goats left footprints
pointed like the olive leaves
the dry leaves rustled
over his broken greaves

233

He was not old
but grey webs of anguish
hung in an immense visage
now growing cold.

SONG

So long my heart
This little polish'd ball of blood
Has throbb'd in unison
With your immortal flood

That now if you should ebb
I'd stay my flow
And sink into the sterile sands
Beneath us bleak and low.

CONSTELLATION

There was a fall as from the sky
It might have been a burning star
We walked like mortals in a street
And up a marble stair. Restless water
Everywhere. Sharp shadows wove
A portent of some change: broke up
The unreal world. There was a bell
A barge of yellow fruit: and at the end
A garden wall: a door which she unlatch'd
To show a room its white walls hung
With trophies from the labyrinth.
And she was there and I was there
And there a bull for sacrifice.

LIVE AND LOVE

A tracery of dispersed veins
sustains the wheeling rose of blood
light transfused myriad-spoked
the conflict of sun and ice

Saving where we should spend
Sleeping in order to dream
And all we find in the end
Is an old boot in the stream

the apex in the ice. The herons
have left the busy vale
Heraclitus in his white robe
has passed us unobserved

Never seek to know your neighbour
Live out of hand love out of need
Let it be your last endeavour
To keep the cold outside the shroud.

INSCRIPTION

(for a book of memories)

Take this book that's but a fable
Told into the icy night:
Think kindly of a man not able
To face the fiery light.

He had wandered over mountains
And bruised his feet on stones
Had dreamt of wine-fed fountains
That dull the ache of bones.

235

Now he is past and gone Madam
His fame has gone before:
It is a ghost of Adam
That knocks upon your door.

SONNET

My hand that out of the silk subsiding waters
Reaches in despair
Might be some shipwrecked mariner's
And the cool soft breast it caresses
The curdled crest of a wave

But a heart beneath beats tranquilly
And her mind is wandering restlessly
Over the wide dominions of sense.

She is free: I know her voice will sing
Above the severed oaks: her steps
Will be light as she proceeds
Festively under a fate
Dark as falling assegai.

She is a nymph and she is free
And I am but a fettered ape.

GALA

(Lago Maggiore)

There was fire on the water that night
Violence and splendour for the common delight
But the stars were false and too slowly fell
To death. Such artifice could not dispel
The sense of endless space, of burning spheres

Expended in a black abyss.

                               When fires
Are lit by physical friction, some trace
Is left as stigmata on the blank face
Of heaven above us.

                       Stars go out, but we
Fretted to this same white intensity
By the harsh collision of our hates and loves
Shine only inwardly. Our little globes
Turn their opaque shells on human eyes
And what is born brightly, darkly lives and dies.

SONNET

This plain is a full arena for any eyes
Outfanning from my feet like a ribbed shell
Its tinctures the interblent haze
Of autumnal moistures. A rocking bell
Peals in a gray tower filling the leafless vales
With felt sound. Falling house-reek
Scatters against the fallow fields
Or drifts into furry woods which break
The sky like black buffaloes bent
To assail the burnish-bellied clouds.
Berries in hedges are splashes spilt
In this massed conflict. Along the roads
Beech-boles evade the shuffling mists
Bearing into vision like sheer masts.

SONNET

One day you will intuitively come
Home again driving westward
Into the burning sun: memory
a dusty screen that blinds the vision
You will wind through the narrow lanes
Over the frequent culverts where willows
Sprout in clumps. The marshes
Remember the marigolds and over the farm
The pines stretch agonised arms
It will be still and you will descend
Into an arena of yellow corn
That not a breath of wind stirs

And a rook if it should swerve in the sky
Will move the whole world momentously.

LU YÜN'S LAMENT

*(Lu Yün was the younger brother of the famous fourth-century
Chinese poet, Lu Chi)*

To be born in the shadow of a mighty oak
    such was my fate
I ran as far as my feet would carry me
    but the black pattern of its branches
        covered my tracks.

I grew in stature
    but high above me was the feathery crown of this tree.
The acorns fell about me
    wild boars fed at my feet.
I had a bright cutlass but the sun never shone on it
    its flash was never seen.

I walked to the North but a bough stretched out before me
   covered with snow.
I walked to the South and was grateful for the shade.
When I came to the West the leaves were already falling on
                        my head.
I turned to the East and found the sun caught in a cage of
                        twigs.

One day the oak will fall
   but whether towards me to bury me
   or away from me to expose me
is still unknown.

Meanwhile I have learned to play my flute softly
   as I lean against the bole of this mighty oak
Or when my fingers are listless
   to listen to the nightingales that sing
      somewhere in the tangled darkness above me.

THE GOLD DISC

An Elegy

I will not tread the old familiar path
   Through watery meads and melancholy woods:
   My autumn air is cool, the stubble crisp
   And edged with frills of crystal frost: my moods
   Are for endurance stript—boughs would break
   Did leaves sustain a falling snow.
   Life's subtlest forms sink to evade
   Wintry storms: blizzards may blow
In vain against the bark, the shell, the seed beneath the sod.

Under a weather'd skin the blood will flow
   The faster in its tried and polish'd bed.
   If limbs have lost their agile fling
   It is because they leapt too far ahead

Striving to gain precarious rest.
Grace is given when flesh and spirit run
In equal pace, two fettled mares
Yoked to a featherweight car. The race is won
On points of style and stateliness—the air is all.

The air is all and ageless—ageless too
The bubbling lymph that makes of man
An animal susceptible to love.
O, not the lust that since the world began
Spawned the race under hedge or roof,
But some remoter essence, drained from this,
That foregoes the natural aim, to weave
Legends of devotion or of mutual bliss—
The never defin'd, the always unrealiz'd pattern of our
                                                    delight.

Why in this dry autumnal season
Should the Castalian wonder never cease?
Why should nerves involuntarily twitch
That had settled to a serene and witless ease?
A face in the amorphous crowd takes shape
Is framed in dark fire and fused
Like bright enamels on the vacant field
Of a mind that was wandering perhaps amused
By the vanity and the variety of an average mundane scene.

Is the response still electrically slick
Or is caution from the first a soft veil
That moderates the shock and restrains
A gesture whose configuration might fail
To register the shape (though not the size)
Of a nascent emotion? Who can say?
In a man imagination and mind
Blend to a unity: a woman may
Shift from mind to instinct, behave like a blind worm.

This instinct drives any one of us on
Like a boat before a wild and refluent wind.

If we are not wrecked on hidden sands or reefs
It is because we are guided by a mind
Bent on measuring distances and depths.
But caution breeds distrust: we are men
To the degree we adventure, lift eyes
From our immediate dead reckoning and then
Carry our load of longing to a haven unvisited.

Safe in this Thule or Trebizond
Sails furl'd and nibbling round the shore
We may then look over the dancing prow
And decide what we could not decide before:
Whether the new has a look of the old,
Whether the deck beneath our feet
Is more solid than the strand over there
Seductively shadow'd as it is for the sweet
Pleasures of love by palm-trees, acacias and rushes.

But we have to take account of crew and cargo
For one may mutiny and the other rot.
Those blustering fellows I have on board
Are restrain'd as they work by the thought
Of ultimate ease, all that wealth can buy
Falter now and they will plot to kill
Their negative captain, scuttle the ship
Make for the shore and enjoy their fill
Of lust and leisure and the momentary whatever-you wish.

Between measure and mood, indecision and deed
We can hover a lifetime. I hover'd with you
And with you and with you—until I retir'd
With my stinking cargo and scowling crew.
I came back to port and now lie in dry dock
With the crew paid off and my hopes curtail'd
But it is odd that I feel no remorse
No sense of a mission that fail'd
As I savour the smoke of the burning leaves, and the acid
                                                    decay.

But that, it will be said, was your physical cruise:
What of the spirit and its search for truth?
Have you found in old age some end
To the quest you began in your youth?
Yes: an end to the restless endeavour
To define what is within or without,
The scope of belief—of unbelief too
For in the end I have put all in doubt
God, man; earth, heaven: I live on in alert suspense.

I believe in my unbelief—would not force
One fibre of my being to bend in the wind
Of determinate doctrine. In doubt there is stillness
The stillness that elsewhere we may find
In the sky above us where the fix'd stars
Mete out infinity and space folds
To contain the secret substance of life
Which time in its tragic furnace moulds
To the forms of grief and glory, of vice and holiness.

But gently, lest the rhetoric steal
This mood of quietness. I will not preach
A private brand of pride or shame.
I too have heard the sounding rivers, the screech
Of amorous winds. But now the night is calm.
I listen to a music fraught with silence
To a solitude full of sound.
I have found the peace beyond violence
And gaze steadily into the gold disc that blurs all hard
                                        distinctions.

NEW POEMS 1965

DAPHNE

Daphne so long attached
to my broken daydreams
with troubadors and bogomils
heresiarchs of all extremes

loosen your limbs and green tresses
from their botanical growth
redeem not your trembling flesh
nor the oval mouth

of your rapturous cry
stay rooted in black earth
but allow your mythical anguish
a miraculous rebirth

In your shade I am the dove
in your leaves the voice of love

2

The secret that you locked
in immobility
is evident in the tremors
of this intricate tree

from leaf to leaf a whisper
falls through the air
my taut intelligent ear
receives each syllable of despair

Slow virginal never torrential
rivers on a pergament map
your veins in many deltas
disperse a perpetual sap

septal pipes through which seep
osmotic fluids that never sleep

3

The god was young and terrible
with toad eyes and goat feet
his voice a gulp that tore a throat
rank with deceit

A hot breath burned her cheek
the hand that wrenched the saffron silk
released one breast that fell aslant
and white as milk

but she was free and fled down paths
where once she'd played with naked boys
as innocent as she—invincible prowess
added to the joys

of days of bland Olympian light
not broken by an earthly night

4

The palsy that possessed her limbs
immobilised each bone
impulsive energies
transformed the girdled zone

From hidden wells within her flesh
a green alchemic flood
began to climb along the veins
and chased the ebbing blood

right to the crimpled finger-tips
To tresses and coy fringes
it introduced a glaucous blush
and intermediate tinges

until her features seem to fade
into a shadow in a shade

5

The god clutched blindly at the twigs
grown lithe or brittle
caressed a branch smooth as a limb
and leaves more crisp and subtle

than any since enured by time
A piercing herbal scent
issued from the ribbed valley
of her wild astonishment

His anguished digitals
bit into the mild bark
the cruel maculations
left their mark

as freckles of a darker green
mottling the trunk's mat even sheen

6

Sick with thwarted lust
Apollo sank on the cotted grass
that covered her groping roots
The blood that in a bolting mass

had pressed against his groins
passed like a veil across his eyes
and a calm occlusion
stifled the little cries

that pursed his bitter lips. How long he lay
we do not know
but when his eyes opened their vertical gaze
was filled with the moon's glow

against which the leaves of the laurel tree
trembled mockingly

7

Rooted Daphne remained: Apollo went
in quest of easier prey
Daphne was rooted but her senses
did not decay

but in the waving wilderness
found their surfeit
voices of innocence to celebrate
the god's defeat

her union with the green
organic wealth of trees
a dialogue with zephyrs
an intercourse with birds and bees

explicit signals of delight
sent out from leaves reflecting light

What Daphne lost in tears and blood
and frenzy of the flesh
you may imagine—I celebrate
the subtler mesh

of innocence and fear
She was not made
for lust and generation
and never sought the deceptive aid

of ogling eyes—in intercourse
her voice of silvery pitch
would penetrate the listening mind
low even inexplicably rich

and there was wedded to the ice
of images crystalline and precise

9

And yet there was no coldness there
but a radiance so intense
that those with whom she held debate
kept a silence

entranced as are astronomers
by a celestial interchange
of fire and frost—the voice of Orpheus
was not so strange

when he charmed the ravening beasts
Daphne enlightened a darker mind
and drove the shadow from the place
where love should be enshrined

I mean the love without a name
it is a love devoid of shame

10

Daphne is still alive
in the perpetual green
of the sacred wood
her druids keen

their holy hymns continuously—requiems
wuther in the hollow boles
of neighbouring oaks—lizards
coiled in puckered holes

emerge to guard the breathing leaves
from lesser worms
and lest her branches should be harmed
all brutal storms

hails and other elemental ills
are diverted by the clumpered hills

11

By love deceived or men rejected
we may frequent this sheltered grove
and listen to the canticles
about us and above

and some who well distinguish
Daphne's argent voice
may then decide that love is vain
in loveless life rejoice

Beyond the reach of sickly lust
and fretful strife
there is a stillness of the flesh
another mode of life

in which the still inquiring mind
a recompense for love may find

12

The stricken leaves that lingered
upon this pendant bough
have by now all fallen
low fallen low

The weasel and the ermine
make a secret lair
in Daphne's tawny roots
and all about the fragrant air

darting wrens and linnets
fill the endless day
with pretty cries and sonnets
that would seem to say—

the nymph that from Apollo fled
lives long after he is dead

TIME & BEING

Wait while I shut the gate
   the wild wind is blowing
      and over the eastern wold
   the leaves of the trees and my tender thoughts
      are toss'd to the angry sea.

We will walk over the fields till we reach
   the bare top of the hill
      where the world spins round like a gambler's wheel
   and we and the sheep and the loose white stones
      must dance on its whirling rim.

Beneath this black and tortured thorn
   let us rest as we take our bearing
      you and I in a universe
   where nothing is unless we utter
      and out of our words comes a Word.

Nothing existed and something is born
   like a lamb on the cold green grass
      our Word is bloody and hardly can stand
   bedraggl'd in wind and bitten by thistle
      a bleat of distress.

But it is ours this weanling cry
   not a thought but a poem
      it came out of the womb where nothing was
   from the empty house of Being
      in the time of another world.

Where the rafters are rough and the floors are bare
   where the walls are blank and no vent
      gives out on the wold or the sea
   and the only sound is the sound we make
      the dole of our wondering lips

The curtains of the night are golden
   the curtains of the day are grey
      we are cast for the trembling labour
   the shudder of pain as we slit the veil
      or die in the caul.

ANY CRUCIFIXION

O what is this encroaching midway
bird-bedraggled darkness but a hood
to hide your sense of loss of clenched dismay?

And what the thin and crooked becks of blood
displayed to drain the delta of your pain
but lace upon the waled and woeful limbs
that led you to this spurious mound again?

They are all gone. The jackal climbs
and watches from a mossy sill.
You are alone unendingly alone
and people slowly walking down the hill
bruise the myrtle on the calcined stone.

AILRED

Ailred awakes in the raw abbey
   to the flare of rivulets
      and the coal effort of the wren
the stript twigs are
   veins of jet in the bruised flesh
      of a dawn

articulate in the organic sighs
   of rot, listless leaves, amused mice
      and the massive
         roll of drencht woods

otters advance
   in silk sheaths splash oilily
     into the cold current

Wherever the word is spoken
   the virgin is there to receive it
     the moonstone a separate fire
      on her bosom
watches an eye
   open to the broken image
     of the white hills and the high
      scatter'd quails

DIRGE

The willows now I do regret
   beside the river Rye
the sappy earth and all
   that faked autumnal fire
cool wounds upon the granular wall
   dried veins that clutch
     the indignant eaves
weep, weep
   for all will fall

as slowly as the yellow leaves
as softly as the silken sleeves
   discarded by a bridal bed
now the bright day is dead
   is dead
and we must sleep
   or die

WINTER DUSK

Rain-filled ruts
reflect
an apple-green sky

Into black huts
a shawled woman
shoos her hissing geese

A cold wind
insinuates
the evening star

Bleak thorns
and wassail berries
hide the sweet thrush

BOWER BIRD

Blest orange crest
Hunstein and Goldie
beak boy and olive-
brown breadwinner

bright basket and bough
black sap and berry
confused inclusion
of crumb and plunder

wispy tunnel
whiteleaf woe
he doles a shrill canticle
uptil a dry thorn

a fabric cone
and Christ why wonder
such telltale cumber
of hormone provender

FERTILE FEATHERS

Feather & weather & the fertile zone
feature forever the mind of God
grace & gristle butcher-bird & bat
distribute the seed by splitting the pod

Mostly the swallow but sometimes the rook
risks the sun's anger by displacing a bud
but broaching the reef comes the gladstone-bag rampant
and restores to the egg its eye of bright blood

IN A PERSIAN GARDEN

The eyes of the philosophers
test the separate
sensations of light and dark
bats cling to the crumbling minarets
and swiftly with his scimitar
the Prince divides
Shivala's silken lashes

From a tulip-tree
the moon's rays
shake into the bright piscina
a withered leaf

Time is blazoned
on a broken shield

255

THE VISIONARY HERMIT

(for Michael Tippett)

Action I have loved
  and the taut rein
the even canter
  along the open ridge

Now the pace slackens
Listlessly hangs the rein
  over the arched neck
    as we descend
      into the green dale

2

A kingfisher
  blue steel under the stone arches
    darts along the beck
      by the abandoned mill

An ancestor of mine lived here
  a century and a half ago
carved his name on the lintel
  and a verse from the Greek bible

built a sundial on a grassy mound
  incised:
    Time and Life move swiftly
    Quod hora est vide

Now the doors are rotted
  the glass in the windows broken
the road obliterated: only the black-faced sheep
  visit this place

the silence substantial
  the millwheel unmoving
the granaries empty
  the wide moors
    an oasis enfolding

a mill at the world's end

Stars glitter
  above the slumbering cattle
    the obliterated farms

Intense remnants of time—in my youth
  I saw the universe as fragmentation
    matter burning in limitless space

I saw myself
  a bud thrusting through black soil
    a point of green fire
      sucked upward by the sun

I thought I could gather
  a unity from the air
that my exfoliated petals
  would radiate from a golden eye

My senses in the soil
my stem an upright channel
my tender twigs
  stretched toward the limits of the glittering sky

The stars have not moved in their stations
  time has become finite
I stare at the twisted tree
  my life

The vanity of artifice
    I have abandoned
the rhyme
    the elegant rhythm

All these vanities belong to the old time
    for men no longer listen

Will men listen again to a new utterance
    the rhythm of the heart
        the true voice of feeling?

Not until the miller returns to the mill
    and the waters grind the corn
        for farms reclaimed from the moor

Not until the cry of the gull
    driven in from the sea
answers in the green dale
    the human ululation

FROM THE PLATFORM

Chasing butterflies is an occupation
not generally despised and leading by devious routes
to an occasional catch and more rarely
to a new discovery and a hasty attempt
at Linnean classification.
But my thoughts as they hover over these conglomerate faces
bedded like pebbles on the floor of the hall
resist the net of attention. Why am I here?
Resolute for what end? My own satisfaction?
Scarcely. The night is wet and foggy—I might have dined
with a congenial friend. But here

we are confederates in a desperate cause
a few the unhappy few
redeemed from apathy, anxious
to save the world from a cindery end.
But why is the world not with us?
Why are these wistful eccentric faces
lifted to words that bring no hope
from lips so vainly rhetorical?

No need to speak, to confess
my illogical emotion and settled despair.
I am here to be helpful. My tactical face
must not betray my strategic doubts.
It is a matter of death or life—
such is my conviction. But now my gaze
rests on a figure I have seen before
a woman huddled apart. She once had a child
I knew it well and saw it white in her arms
sleeping for ever after a night of pain.
But that was long ago—she is not here to mourn.
The butterfly swoops on this dusky bloom
and my net descends. What has it caught?
Pity and terror, a memory, and the seed
that was joy and that still
might quicken the torpid heart.

The chairman is tapping the table
the rouser is begging for funds
justice and peace are not cheap
bills to be printed appeals to be mailed.
Our eloquence is nearly exhausted and soon
we shall scatter in the streets and merge
with the indifferent crowd.
                              And what was achieved?
An evening of mortification, a gesture of defiance and grace?
I do not know. My net is folded and aslant the light
soft needles of rain assault my defenceless face.

COBDEN

COBDEN imperturbably stone
divides the flow of Camden traffic
frock-coated elevated stiff alone
—it is an academic trick
(petrification of the flesh
façade of an impassive mind)

Collisions happen in the milling mesh
to which we humans are consigned
but COBDEN neither sees nor feels
our common fate
nor hears the rumble of the wheels
early or late

VOCAL AVOWALS

Experiments

—Est-ce exact, *demanda Degas à Mallarmé*, que dans l'un de vos sonnets, les meilleurs de vos exegétès voient, les uns un crépuscule, d'autres une aurore, les autres l'absolu? Quand ils ont sollicité du Maître le mot de l'énigme, ne leur avez-vous pas répondu: c'est ma commode! —

HENRI MONDOR, *Vie de Mallarmé*,
Gallimard, éditeur

basic black

(to alberto burri)

cry crew cry memory florida
masterly most crimson silt
shy masculine myrtle endeavour
sever christ cavalier host
ghost gonads sob linger
alleys lost singular wing
veins of love never ever cease
keep crestfallen thy cruise
dastard sap till sessions eventual
mortal leman entrance dry
wild hollow winter bruises
droop vocal illyrian avowals
kiss merciful o homily thy keel
england vesicles of delight
lost ever ever ever white pyx
residues of lust ah wax lack

asp

lunar last
crisp sting

lace leaf
thy down

when solent
shy eskimos

charred tents
the tender

263

breast pastures
crust under

sovereign silk waterfalls
listen the

khaki clamour of
clustered acorns

and thy tiny
crisp
        blueberry sense

then wake
    lest the odalisk
    die cold

silk wrist

gross funicular gilt
waste icicle gun lea
hurtle glass low linger
so delicate call clasp
cast finger cool column
no drum clam drastic
hollow coronal all ice
false fire cloud o' maul
memory now milk

cradle song

shell leaf lifania
leaf kiss condone
trident syllabic
system restrain

marlowe meridian
lissom lodore
buddha barbaria
now alone

sound look

behaglich glitter gum gladly
ghost of serpentine silverly
lost when webern vast
dealt dolmens sheer separate
slither so soon
to redound

best night

yule dungeon
dry drained
docile dingle

dragoon gust
fell fable
rest iris

belle jaune
blue gong
kale candle

climb cling
  beverley moon
  dry crest

or organ

simply say softly well welter
tennis effort ex- if not
lustless bones thy river
red snow repeat milk sting
stagger hock cry cluster
oosh and then curls wait
sweat sweet silver wheat
white lintel
o'er

fur matrix

(*for etienne martin*

lob west weld needle
seed slight blue suck
settle far consecrate
white angel wistful

margaret melt
anvil muster for
wonderfully far
black mutter

rose llama
lustre syndrome
tell pelvic tell tower
matrix murmur

mason bee

melon vulvular vast
tax tintagel
try tone lax sigh
archangel fore lost
may duke may die
well rent infest
oak eye

fellow men

sharl rumble enlist while
crumble distress coarse foal
belt so wormeaten whine
wold zithers wet fear

rode alabastrine sheer built
till install aisle coomb
vivid surrender up black
up cry up coign

in lily lake tangents
zion wonder and wound
cusped blood tellurian
transit illicit wild

wry fling test modesty
fell yolk
folk mold
goddam yellow

little war

geometric my alkahest
migrant fists passion vale
flash high o paraclete
all violet vast
eyelashes entelechy
stone water-swords
white shock

hot rod

vellum list fell dole
packed pendulum red roar
esteem wet spindle
auricular thy lung
scut thews cold selvage
out angular out out odd
yet not

petals

liquid wild black lance
levret dapple drencht
all orchid mast
B U T glance
thy sense thy dog thy
black lips fastuous immortal
fell ochre ice ink
white dust dog dam
welling metals

WHAT IS A POEM?

WHAT IS A POEM?

Some years ago I was invited to give a graduate seminar on poetry at Princeton University. Some very distinguished American scholars honoured me by their presence, among them a philosopher for whose work I already had a great admiration—Susanne Langer. In the discussions that followed my paper week by week Mrs Langer would almost always end by asking: 'But what is a poem? You have told us what poetry is, and so have many other critics of the past and present, but no one will tell me what a poem is.'

At the time I felt that the distinction Mrs. Langer wanted to make was a little pedantic, but the more I have thought about it since, the more relevant it has become, not only to the theoretical discussion of poetry, but to my own practice as a poet.

In effect, Mrs. Langer was asking me to distinguish between the material of an art and the 'work' into which that material is wrought. The distinction is easy enough to grasp in the plastic arts—the painter does not, as a normal practice, paint without a methodical procedure directed towards *containing* his activity, setting it within the predetermined limits of a canvas or a mural panel. The modern poet, with few exceptions, writes poetry as if he were taking his Muse for a walk and gives up when he feels tired or falls behind the Muse. Even when he is using the aids of a traditional metre or formal measure, he takes these in his stride—he paces out a distance that has no necessary limit.

What else can he do? He can enter a maze or a labyrinth; he can keep to the paths of a formal garden. That is what might be called the academic procedure, followed by poets who still write sonnets. But this is not necessarily to write *a poem* in Mrs. Langer's sense of the term. Not every sonnet is a poem, any more than every cabinet picture is a painting. The poem, even when it has some predetermined pattern, must be wrought to some effect or finish that justifies the exclamation: This is a poem!

In my critical writings I have often spoken about 'organic

form', circling in an unsystematic way about the question asked by Mrs Langer. There is a sense in which the form of a work of art is as complete (and as imperfect when not complete) as the form of a flower or a fruit. How can the poet achieve such a sense of perfect form?

Not by taking pains to that end. The achievement is nothing if not spontaneous: a perfection of silent growth, a point of maturity, a ripeness in the fruit that reaches a limit and then falls into the lap of the waiting consumer. Aestheticians may be able to give us some indications of this optimum condition of *being*, but indications only. In poetry it would seem to be essentially a question of rhythm, but, we might also ask: what is a rhythm? Conventionally a rhythm is identified with one or another of those traditional 'measured flows' of syllables, those various metres known as iambic, dactylic, trochaic, etc. If a critic can identify such measures in a poet's work it is said to be rhythmical. But the rhythm of a poem, and indeed rhythm in general, is a much more complex problem. 'Rhythmic speech or writing', to quote H. W. Fowler's *Modern English Usage*, 'is like waves of the sea, moving onward with onward rise and fall, connected yet separate, like but different, suggestive of some law, too complex for analysis or statement, controlling the relations between wave and wave, waves and sea, phrase and phrase, phrases and speech . . . Metre is measurement, rhythm is flow, a flow with pulsations as infinitely various as the shape and size and speed of the waves, and infinite variety is not amenable to tabulation such as can be applied to metre.' A rhythm in verse is an organic flow of a group of words, differing from prose rhythm only in its closed configuration (its end is in its beginning), in its tenser structure, in its separate identity. Whether the poet regulates such a rhythm by an imposed measure is a matter of choice: a particular measure being one of an infinite number of rhythms.

We often, in all the arts, speak of the fitness of a form to its content, and the fitness of a form in verse is the conformity of its rhythmical structure to the poem's content.

But what is the content of a poem? The words are not necessarily arranged in a logical order whose primary purpose is to communicate a meaning of some kind (if by meaning we mean a verifiable statement or proposition). The words in a poem (it might be more exact to speak of the syllables in a poem) are vocal signs that convey an intangible essence (the 'pattern' of a feeling), an essence that vanishes the moment we approach it with our analytical intelligence. The rhythmical pattern corresponds in some mysterious way with the inner feeling, and the rhythm ceases the moment the feeling loses its intensity, its 'virtue'. But meanwhile the rhythm has captured the feeling, held it in a crystal cage. There it remains as an image, sealed and immortalized for our contemplation. We have caught beauty in a wild foray, as I say in one of my poems, and that is all we are required to do. The form we have created is now remote from the emotion we experienced.

The poem is a rhythmical figure, complete in itself, but the poet may find it difficult to detach such a figure of speech from the language of daily discourse, a language worn and debased by centuries of prosaic usage. The great modern heresy in poetry is to confuse the use we make of words in a poem with the modalities of speech. Poetry has no essential need of the grammatical structure or topical idioms we use in the communication of meaning.

True poetry was never speech, but always song. Modern poetry, in so far as it aspires to establish the integral form of a poem, is a refinement of song—a containment of our symbols of discourse in a singular melody. A melody is an organic 'round' of sound corresponding in its finiteness to the feeling that is 'realized' at the moment of utterance. The rhythm of a poem is this melody or cadence that rises and falls with a rhythmical articulation. A poem is therefore to be defined as a structure of words whose sound constitutes a rhythmical unity, complete in itself, irrefragable, unanalyzable, completing its symbolic references within the ambit of its sound-effect.

It will be noted that this definition of a poem does not

require in a poem a verifiable meaning, an intellectual or moral or social communication. A poem is not a statement, but a manifestation, a manifestation of *being*. It may be that some poems are enhanced by a meaning, but I have never been able to discover what difference the inclusion of a verifiable meaning made to any poem that spontaneously suggests itself to the mind as archetypal, such as one of Shakespeare's songs. Many great poets take occasion, in writing a poem, to be philosophical or social critics or entertainers, and they have great ability in these ambiguous roles; but Ariel's song rises mockingly above their cares and is 'no mortal business, nor no sound that the earth owes'. Poetry, we might say, is concerned with the truth of what is, not with what is truth. Heidegger says that 'poetry is the saga of the unconcealment of what is.'

This conception of the poem was held, not always very expressly, by the poets who were my immediate mentors, by T. E. Hulme, F. S. Flint, Ezra Pound, H. D., T. S. Eliot, Marianne Moore and William Carlos Williams. This new poetic awareness was for a short time called Imagism, and as such was accused of triviality and incoherence; but it is possible to be aware of the true nature of a poem and yet to achieve its essential integrity only rarely. I believe that the poets I have mentioned have written the only certainly perdurable poems in our century, and that poets like W. B. Yeats in his later work and even Robert Frost in his best work were influenced by their example. But I have no wish to be partisan on this occasion. I have written these few pages in an attempt to explain what I myself understand a poem to be. I have not been consistent in my own practice, and most of the poems in this volume, which represent the frugal total of a life's work, are deficient by my own standards. But I believe that a few of them do satisfy these standards because my often repeated consideration of their form has left them intact. These few poems, which the fallibility of my own judgement forbids me to name, I dedicate to the Muse of Pure Poetry.

H.R.

NOTES

The poems are printed as groups in the order of their first publication in separate volumes, but a few poems hitherto uncollected have been inserted in their approximate chronological sequence. 'New Poems, 1965' and 'Vocal Avowals' have not hitherto appeared in separate volumes, though some of the New Poems were printed in *Selected Writings* (1963). A few minor revisions have been made in the previously published texts.

This collection includes in their final form all the poems which the author wishes to preserve.

NOTES

Page 13   *Eclogues* was first published in a limited edition (200 copies) by the Beaumont Press (London), the cover and the decorations designed by Ethelbert White, the typography and binding arranged by Cyril Beaumont. The colophon states that it was 'completed December the Twentieth MDCCCCXIX', but the poems had been written and delivered to the Press at least two years earlier.

Page 27   *Naked Warriors* was published by *Art and Letters* at 9 Duke Street, Adelphi, London, in 1919. It was printed at the Pelican Press and had a cover design by Wyndham Lewis. On the title-page the following epigraph was printed:

'And there were some that went into battle naked and unarmed, fighting only with the fervour of their spirit, dying and getting many wounds'.

The volume also contained the following 'Preface':

'I would like to speak for a new generation to the following effect:

'We, who in manhood's dawn have been compelled to care not a damn for life or death, now care less still for the convention of glory and the intellectual apologies for what can never be to us other than a riot of ghastliness and horror, of inhumanity and negation.' May we, therefore, for the sake of life itself, be resolved to live with a cleaner and more direct realisation of natural values. May we be unafraid of our frank emotions, and may we maintain a callous indifference to the falsely-artistic prettifying of life. Then, as the reflex of such stern activity, may we strive to create a beauty where hitherto it has had no absolute existence. From the sickness of life revealed let us turn with glad hearts to the serenity of some disinterested beauty. In that way we may so progress that our ethical rage give us duly an aesthetic sanction.'

The poems in this volume also were written some time before the date of publication, most of them in the years 1916-17.

Pages 47-52 The first three of these hitherto uncollected poems were written in 1915-16, before the full impact of war had been felt. 'Auguries of Life and Death' was an immediate reaction to the news of the death of the poet's brother, who was killed in action on 5th October, 1918.

Page 53 *Mutations of the Phoenix* was printed and published by Leonard & Virginia Woolf at The Hogarth Press, Hogarth House, Richmond, in 1923. It had the following epigraph printed after the title-page:

'Life is complex in its expression, involving more than percipience, namely desire, emotion, will, and feeling. It exhibits variations of grade, higher and lower, such that the higher grade presupposes the lower for its very existence. This suggests a closer identification of rhythm as the casual counterpart of life; namely, that wherever there is some rhythm, there is some life, only perceptible to us when the analogies are sufficiently close. The rhythm is then the life, in the sense in which it can be said to be included within nature.'

A. N. WHITEHEAD: *The Principles of Natural Knowledge*

Page 75 'Beata l'alma' was originally entitled 'Monologue addressed to a wondering Tyro.'

Collected Poems 1913-25 (published by Faber & Gwyer, London, 1926) had the following epigraphs:

'*Le Phenix n'a point de ſexe ny de pareil; il aime hautement & en lieu où il ne peut toucher que des yeux; il n'y a que de l'intelligence & de la lumiere, en ce qui'il aime; & s'il se brusle à cette lumiere, c'est ſur un bucher de canelle, c'est d'vn feu innocent qui ne le tourmente poinr, & qui ne luy fait point de fumée. Nous ſommes auertis par là, d'éleuer nos affections au deſſus de corps & de la masse: de ne leur ſouffrir rien de material que ce qui peut entrer par les yeux: de ne viſer qu'à ce beau abstrait & à ce lumineux dégagé, qui éclaire ce qu'il échauffe, & qui purifie ce qu'il attire: de n'admettre aucun feu qui ne ſoit d'enhaut & de bonne odeur: & pour abreger cette Philoſophie en vn mot, d'aimer auſſi purement, que ſi nous eſtions faits comme ces Cherubins qui n'ont que les aiſles & la teſte.*

Ie ne m'enflame que de lumiere

Sans ſexe comme ſans pareil,
   Ie ne prens feu qu'aux rayons du Soleil;
   Et de ma mort ie fais ma vie.
Mon tourment est illustre, & mon feu parfumé;
   Et par vn amour digne & d'honneur & d'envie,
   Ie ſuis chaste & ſuis enflamé.

DEVISES HEROIQVES ET MORALES DV. P. PIERRE LE MOINE de la Compagnie de IESVS.   1649.

'*Obscurity in affection of words and indigested conceits, is pedantical and childish; but where it shroudeth itself in the heart of his subject, uttered with fitness of figure and expressive epithets, with that darkness will I still labour to be shadowed.*'

GEORGE CHAPMAN: Epistle Dedicatory to OVID'S BANQUET OF SENSE.

Page 113   The following note was placed at the end of the first and all subsequent printings of *The End of a War*:

'It was necessary for my poetic purpose to take an incident from the War of 1914-18 which would serve as a focus for feelings and sentiments otherwise diffuse. The incident is true, and can be vouched for by several witnesses still living. But its horrors do not accuse any particular nation; they are representative of war and of human nature in war. It is not my business as a Poet to condemn war (or, to be more exact, modern warfare). I only wish to present the universal aspects of a particular event. Judgment may follow, but should never precede or become embroiled with the act of poetry. It is for this reason that Milton's attitude to his Satan has so often been misunderstood.'

Pages   'Love and Death' and 'A Dream' are printed
141-5   and discussed in *Collected Essays in Literary Criticism* (1938), pages 106, 111-14. 'The Death of a Statesman' originally appeared in *The New Statesman*.

Page 149   'Bombing Casualties in Spain' was occasioned by a newspaper photograph of children killed in the Spanish Civil War, 1936.

Page 150   Herschel Grynszpan was a Polish Jew aged seventeen who assassinated Ernst von Rath, third secretary of the German Embassy in Paris, on November 7, 1938. The event was followed by violent pogroms in Central Europe.

Page 181   The 1953 edition of *Collected Poems* has the following epigraph:

> Als ob der Schmerz denn etwas andres wär
> Als dieses ewige Dran-denken-müssen,
> Bis es am Ende farblos wird und leer . . .
> So lass mich nur in den Gedanken wühlen,

Denn von den Leiden und von den Genüssen
Hab längst ich abgestreift das bunte Kleid,
Das um sie webt die Unbefangenheit,
Und einfach hab ich schon verlernt zu fühlen.

HOFMANNSTHAL: *Der Tod des Tizian*

Page 226   Peter Kropotkin, 'the anarchist prince', returned to Russia after the revolution of 1917 and died in disillusionment at Dmitrov near Moscow on the 8th February, 1921. Emma Goldman attended his funeral. This poem was suggested by her description of the event.

Page 228   'Scardanelli' was the name sometimes assumed by the poet Hölderlin in his madness.

Page 230   Kalamis was a famous Athenian sculptor of the fifth century; Sosandra a model of great beauty. Cf. Lucian, *Dialogues of the Hetairai*, III. 2. All that is known of them will be found in *The Sculpture and Sculptors of the Greeks*, by Gisela M. A. Richter, Yale University Press, 1930, pp. 201-5.

Page 231   According to Lemprière, Sappho's 'tender passions were so violent that some have represented her attachments to three of her female companions, Anactoria, Atthis, and Megara, as criminal, and, on that account, have given her the surname of *Tribas*.'

Page 261   Some of these experimental poems first appeared in *Encounter* (March 1959).

INDEX OF FIRST LINES

Gather or take fierce degree, 136
Gently she climbs, 231
geometric my alkahest, 268
gross funicular gilt, 264
Grotesque patterns of blue-gray mould, 16

Haulms burn, 117
He had made no history: no song, 233
He is SaintMichael of the flaming sword, 95
Her angel flight from cliff to lake, 144
Here where I labour hour by hour, 183
His body is smashed, 34
His russet coat and gleaming axe, 17
His wild heart beats with painful sobs, 35
Hylas, the world's perceptual scene, 78

I can just see the distant trees, 15
Ich sterbe. . . . Life ebbs with an easy flow, 101
I have assumed a conscious sociability, 20
In Bednib's shop I picked up a book, 137
In this extensive gloom, 127
In measure and in marksmanship, 178
I, Orm the son of Gamal, 177
I, said the moon, who have been a maiden, 83
I speak not from my pallid lips, 105
I too was present, 130
I wake: I am alive: there is a bell, 109
I will not tread the old familiar path, 239

Leave Helen to her lover, Draw away, 89
Levels ledges, 126
Life so brief . . ., 23
Like a faun my head uplifted, 18
Limbs, 96
liquid wild black lance, 268
lob west weld needle, 266
lunar last, 263

melon vulvular vast, 267
Melville fell, 126
Mute figures with bowed heads, 37
My hand that out of the silk subsiding waters, 236

O dark eyes, I am weary, 17
On a strange bed, I drop my tired head, 141
One day you will intuitively come, 238